Outlaw Tales of Utah

True Stories of Utah's Most Famous Rustlers, Robbers, and Bandits

Michael Rutter

TWODOT

GUILFORD, CONNECTICUT
HELENA, MONTANA

AN IMPRINT OF THE GLOBE PEQUOT PRESS

To my father, Paul Rutter,
who passed away before this book was published

A · T W O D O T® · B O O K

Library of Congress Cataloging-in-Publication Data
Rutter, Michael, 1953–
    Outlaw tales of Utah / Michael Rutter.—1st ed.
      p. cm.
    Includes bibliographical references (p.) and index.
    ISBN 978-0-7627-2427-7
      1. Outlaws—Utah—History—Anecdotes. 2. Outlaws—Utah—Biography—Anecdotes. 3. Utah—History—Anecdotes. 4. Utah—Biography—Anecdotes. 5. Frontier and pioneer life—Utah—Anecdotes. I. Title.

F826.6 .R88 2002
364.1'092'2792—dc21   2002029906

Manufactured in the United States of America
First Edition/Sixth Printing

Contents

Introduction

Few characters in the American West have captured our collective imagination like the outlaws of Utah, specifically Butch Cassidy and the Wild Bunch. Indeed, many of these historical characters have become larger than life.

Somewhere inside our rich western mythology, folklore, and historical accounts is the real truth. Unfortunately, an exact accounting will never be known. These men and women, however interesting, functioned outside the law. They spent a great deal of time and effort covering their tracks. This makes it difficult for those of us interested in their lives a hundred and some years later to root out the details needed to compose completely accurate biographical sketches of their activities.

If you become a student of the outlaws from Utah's early days, you'll discover a plethora of stories and tales. You'll also find that many facts and details were purposely masked, not only to protect the outlaws but also to shield the honest folks (and there were many) who were more than willing to aid and abet. In spite of their crimes, many of the outlaws in this book were beloved by the local people. Butch Cassidy, for example, is rarely, if ever, condemned in legend and seems to have loomed larger than life even long before he hung up his outlaw spurs.

As you'd expect, there are a number of contradictions making it nearly impossible to separate fact from legend and folk mythology. Even firsthand narratives and supposedly accurate historical accounts are seldom in agreement.

The lack of conclusive information is both frustrating and stimulating. It makes it difficult, if not downright impossible, to write a truly accurate account of what actually happened. At the same time, it encourages a desire for more research and creative speculation on what may have taken place. At best, a collector of such tales must deal with the contradictions. Nevertheless, at least on a metaphoric level, the true spirit of the Utah outlaws lives on, and their tales are fascinating to learn.

Butch Cassidy
The Robin Hood Outlaw

Butch was certain no one was following him. Nevertheless, he stopped and wiped the sweat from his brow while he studied the back trail with field glasses. After a quarter of an hour, he was satisfied. Pushing on into the afternoon sun, he saw a rundown ranch. It had been a day since he'd eaten, and he was hungry. Maybe he could ride down and get a meal. When he came to the front door, an elderly couple greeted him. Following the custom of the day, they invited the dusty traveler in for supper. The gray-haired woman put coffee on to boil and wiped a few tears when she thought the stranger was not looking.

"This might be our last afternoon at the place," the rancher explained. "It's really hard on the lady."

The man who held the note on their ranch was due to arrive anytime, and he was going to evict them since they couldn't make the mortgage—cattle prices were down, and it had been a bad year with the drought. The couple had mistakenly assumed that Butch was the bank man before he rode in close. The woman started to cry more openly as her husband talked. Butch had seconds, and she filled his coffee cup. Butch asked how much they needed to clear the note.

The couple explained that they owed the banker five hundred dollars, but it might as well have been five million.

Butch smiled and wiped his mouth and thanked them for the fine meal. As he left, he laid a wad of dirty bills on the table and made the couple take it. Then he asked what the banker looked like and what direction he'd be coming from. Butch told the rancher to get a signed receipt from the man, stressing that this was very important.

Butch Cassidy

Wyoming State Archives

The couple agreed. The woman hugged him. The stranger hadn't told the pair his name, but they knew who he was. He was the famous outlaw they'd heard so much about. Butch rode off, but then he circled back toward Hanksville. The elderly couple reminded him of his own folks, and he reflected over the hard times they'd had trying to make a home in this arid land. He missed his family, but with a price on his head, he didn't get home very often. Besides, he was a little bit ashamed of the life he had chosen.

Butch smoked a cowboy cigarette and waited in the rocks where he could keep an eye on the dirt track. A short time later, a man in a black suit and a string tie rode past and went up to the cabin. Before long, he rode back down the trail heading to town. After he'd gone a couple of miles from the ranch, Butch trotted up to the man and pointed a cocked Colt at his chest. He took back his five hundred dollars in dirty bills, plus the odd notes the man had, and rode off to his hideout. He never did like banks and the mortgage men who ran them.

Another time when Butch Cassidy was on the run, he visited a Chicago sporting establishment that employed a flock of "soiled doves." He was intimately acquainted with one of the girls. The misdirected maiden told the young, dashing outlaw her life story—about how she'd come to such a tragic circumstance and that she wanted, God willing, to leave this path of sin and go back to the West Coast and start all over. She wanted to go straight, get honest, find a nice guy, settle down, have kids, build a white picket fence about her cottage—and leave her past behind.

Butch was touched by the girl's story. He bought her a ticket to Seattle and gave her the last of his money so she could start a new life. It seemed that Butch Cassidy, king of the outlaws and master robber, had a heart of gold under that rough, windblown exterior. It seemed, too, that while he was an outlaw who held people up with a naked Colt .45 and took their money, there must have been some truth to the overly romanticized stories that followed him in his day—and are still part of the folklore today.

In many ways Butch Cassidy was larger than life when he rode the West. He was nice to children and animals. He was generous and kind to the hard-working people he rubbed shoulders with. There are too many accounts of Butch giving someone his last dollar to be completely ignored. And like another mythic legend of yore, Robin Hood of Sherwood Forest, Butch mostly directed his crimes at the rich who tended to prey upon the working class. He never completely shook off his Mormon heritage, even though he associated with murderers and thieves.

He saw himself as a man of the people, if not a man of contradictions. He lived by the gun, but he preached against violence among his fellows. While he was very quick on the draw and apparently a dead-on shot, he claimed that he never killed anyone—nor is there any record that he did. He liked the fast life, but he also liked to lose himself in a library and read for days. He was an outlaw with a conscience, with a morality, or some semblance of morality, especially when compared to others in his profession—he seems to be the epitome of a good guy who did bad things. As a result, he has never failed to capture the public's curiosity—then as well as now. And his legend has only grown.

Butch Cassidy was born Robert LeRoy Parker on April 13, 1866, in Beaver, Utah. He was the first of twelve children in a devout Mormon family. His family called him Roy. His paternal grandfather, Robert Parker, had left Preston, England, after becoming a convert to the Church of Jesus Christ of Latter-day Saints (Mormons). Robert eagerly made his way to the United States, where he crossed the Great Plains with his family, including Roy's father, Max. The Parkers arrived with the Handcart Company, reaching the Salt Lake Valley in the early fall. Roy's mother, Ann Gillies, crossed the plains with the ill-fated Martin-Willy Handcart Company. This wagon train unwisely left too late in the season and was caught in frigid storms in Wyoming. Many of the party perished in the elements—one of the great tragedies of the great migration. Being a little too eager to get to the Promised Land, they paid a high price.

Since both Max and Ann had helped pull handcarts across the plains, they felt a deep sense of pride in their religious beliefs. They were cut from tough pioneer stock. They brought up their children on firsthand stories of the plains and expected strict devotion to the faith they'd nearly died for. (Even under ideal circumstances, pulling and pushing a crude handcart with all one's possessions over 1,000 miles of rough country from Iowa to the Great Basin was quite a feat.) They had sacrificed a great deal for their God and they taught their children to appreciate their rich heritage.

Both parents also valued a good education, and young Roy learned his school lessons well. But in spite of their best efforts, their oldest son strayed from the true teachings of the faith, breaking his mother's heart by becoming one of the most famous, or infamous, outlaws of the American West. Nevertheless, Roy would never completely abandon his heritage or fully exorcise many of the fundamental teachings he learned at Ann's knee. He never lost his respect for the working class, and he hated injustice.

The Parkers lived in Beaver until Roy was about twelve. They fell on hard times and moved to Circleville, where they did well for a short time. Like so many settlers, though, they were nearly driven under by the harsh winter of 1879. Ann reluctantly left her young family to earn money at the nearby Marshall Ranch. She was allowed to keep some eggs and butter for her own use. To earn a bit more for the struggling family, young Roy, who had just entered his teens, worked on the ranch with his mother.

The ranch employed a rough crowd of men, and young Roy naturally idolized them. Ann tried to shelter her boy from the worldly influences of this godless crowd. Young Roy proved to be a hard worker and a first-rate cowhand. He was likable, smart, and quick. At fourteen he was able to do the work of a man without complaint. He quickly won the approval of the older hands and was accepted as a promising cowhand apprentice. A wild, young cowboy named Mike Cassidy took Roy under his wing.

At first Ann was pleased with how her Roy was fitting in as a ranch hand. The lad was accepted by the other men and was earning his way. It was nice, too, for Ann to have a member of her family with her. She got lonely being away from home for five or six days at a time. However, before long she noticed that her little man was changing too quickly. She stepped in and took him back to town to live with the rest of the family, but it was too late. Her son wanted to be a cowboy.

Roy worshipped Mike Cassidy and wanted to be like him. Not only did the likable Mike Cassidy have some rough habits that the strict Mormon Ann disapproved of, it was rumored that he did more than cowboy work at the ranch. He had too much money. His guns, his horse, his saddle, his clothes were a little too fancy for an honest ranch hand to afford. It was rumored that he rode the outlaw trail, that he rustled cattle and horses and sold them in Colorado. This was not the kind of man she wanted her boy looking up to. Ann hoped she'd taught her firstborn right from wrong, so he'd make his own choice and it would be the right one.

That Mike looked upon the young Roy with a great deal of affection—like a younger brother or a son—is obvious. Like all cowhands, Mike took great pride in his skills and passed them on. Roy's hero taught him how to ride, rope, shoot, and quick draw. He even gave his young protégé a saddle. Mike taught the young Parker the finer points of being a cattleman and the art of judging horseflesh—skills Roy would never lose. In his heart, the future Butch Cassidy was always a rancher. He became a superb horseman and rider. He would later ride in a number of races and would be sought after as a jockey. He would also race for his life when the stakes were high.

It turned out that Ann was right: Mike Cassidy was engaged in some serious rustling—his day job was really a cover. He was the head of a successful group of thieves called the Cassidy Gang. No doubt these moonlighting skills were passed down—little was lost on his clever young understudy. After the lad's skills were up to par, he surely rode with Mike's men on their moonlight raids. Mike Cassidy probably wasn't taking livestock from the Marshall Ranch or any nearby ranches. In fact, most evidence suggests that some of the Marshall family and the Marshall hands, including a few local ranchers, had formed a working cooperative for dealing with livestock that had "questionable" brands. They were building up a herd to sell.

Mike Cassidy was skilled at picking up livestock that didn't belong to him, then covering up the trail. In all fairness, a number of the head he took probably weren't branded. They were free stock getting fat in the local draws and canyons. He was a fine stockman and an expert with the red-hot saddle ring, used to brand cattle in the field.

Ann and Max did what they could for LeRoy, but it wasn't enough. Their son left home for good in 1884.

Roy took his first drink of Old Crow—which became his favorite whiskey—his first smoke, and his first chew on the Marshall Ranch. He likely learned, too, about the fairer sex, including women of questionable virtue—albeit secondhand. Although he eventually became the most famous outlaw in Utah, and one of the most famous outlaws in the West, he retained many of his traditional values. He knew the difference between right and wrong, but he couldn't resist financial shortcuts. He vowed that he'd never be poor like his parents.

He changed his name to Butch to protect his parents' reputation. At different times of his life he went by George Cassidy, James Ryan, and Butch Cassidy. He used the name Cassidy in honor of his friend Mike Cassidy. The name Butch came a little bit later—probably when he worked as a butcher in Rock Springs, Wyoming, since a lot of butchers were called Butch.

Butch was a bold, good-looking man who made a good impression. He was just under 5 feet, 11 inches tall. His frequent smile was broad on his square face. He was reckless, but he was smart, and he knew how far to push and when to back off. He liked people, ranchers, farmers, and Indians, and they liked him—liked him a lot. They protected him as one of their own, which often made the difference between capture and escape. He tipped his hat to the ladies. He was rarely drunk or disorderly. He made friends easily.

While he strayed from the faith of his youth and the fundamental teachings of Mormonism, he had a strong work ethic. And although he was a thief, his word was good, and he was a devoted friend.

In June 1889, Butch crossed the line, entering the world of serious crime. Up until this point, his offenses had been petty by comparison. He had been involved in the rustling trade, but that was considered a minor, if not a forgivable, offense. He fell in with Tom McCarty, a regional, small-time outlaw; Bert Madden, a former bartender; and Matt Warner, a small-time rustler from Brown's Hole (in the northeastern corner of Utah). The four started off as drinking buddies and became good friends who all shared an interest in racehorses.

The group raced three horses in the Four Corners area rather successfully and were involved in petty rustling and petty theft. But they had higher ambitions. They wanted to get rich quickly. Butch was familiar with the setup of the San Miguel Valley Bank in Telluride, Colorado. He had been to Telluride many times. McCarty was the leader of the planned caper, since he had the most experience, but all were eager participants.

Above all, they wanted a big score. The McCarty Gang, as they were called, held up the bank and rode off with a cool $10,500. But they were recognized as they left town, and they became wanted men. Their lives would never be the same again.

The robbery had been well planned—they accounted for contingencies. McCarty had insisted that they use only the best horses—including fresh horses along the escape path—since their lives would depend upon them. This was a lesson the young Butch would never forget. They fled for their lives, trusting entirely in their fine mounts. Central Utah was too hot to hide out in, so they headed north where the winters were colder (and the climate healthier for men with a price on their heads).

McCarty's brother, Bill, and Bill's son, Fred, joined the gang. They weren't so lucky and were later killed in Delta, Colorado, trying to rob the Merchant's Bank. Apparently, at this point Tom McCarty learned his lesson, took his money, and escaped, dropping into semiretirement. Butch's appetite for the high life was only whetted.

He hung out in Brown's Hole, working on ranches and quietly living off his share of the Telluride loot. He actually considered going straight. It is reported that he even worked at the huge Swan Land and Cattle Company. But old habits are hard to break. He went back into business for himself—rustling cattle and horses, trying to build up a herd—but he drew some bad luck. He bought a horse ranch near the Wind River Mountains with Al Hainer (sometimes spelled Rainer). Along with Al, he was caught in 1893 with horses he hadn't paid for.

The case came to trial the following year. Al was acquitted, but Butch was found guilty and sentenced to two years in prison. He was a model prisoner. After serving eighteen months, he asked if he might be paroled since he'd served a good deal of his sentence. It seems the warden was impressed with Butch and said, "You're smart enough to make a success in almost any field. Will you give me your word that you will quit rustling?"

Butch reportedly said, "I can't do that, sir, because if I gave you my word, I'd have to break it. I'm in too deep to quit this game. But I'll promise you one thing: If you pardon me, I'll not rustle in Wyoming."

After being released from prison, Butch headed toward Wyoming's Hole-in-the-Wall, where he hooked up with Flat Nose Curry, Bub Meeks, Elza Lay, and Kid Curry. After a reunion of sorts, they headed down to Brown's Hole to plan their next job.

For the next few years, trains and banks drew their special focus. Butch would give new meaning to the term *organized crime*. Rustling would become less important. The Union Pacific was especially hard hit. Within a few years, nearly every law enforcement agency in the West was homing in on Butch's gang. The Pinkertons would become especially problematic—they would not give up. By the early part of 1900, Butch Cassidy had been a professional outlaw for nearly twelve years, and it was wearing him down. The heyday of outlawing in the West was about over. During his career, he had spent two years in prison, he had thrown some wild parties, and had played hard, but he had almost nothing to show for it. The constant pressure put on him and the Wild Bunch by law enforcement was too much. There were too many close calls, too many days on the trail freezing and roasting, eating only half-cooked beans, if that. His former strongholds, Brown's Hole, Robber's Roost, Hole-in-the-Wall, had all been compromised.

In this frame of mind, Butch made a bold move. He considered going straight and wanted to make a deal. Butch's so-called Train Robbers Syndicate was posing serious problems to banks and railroads—especially the Union Pacific. The famous outlaw contacted Judge O. W. Powers and explained his desire to start over. The judge was convinced that Butch wanted to change his life, so convinced, in fact, that he personally contacted Utah governor Herbert Wells. Governor Wells finally met with Butch, who asked for amnesty from his offenses. After all, he had never killed a man during the commission of his crimes. After a frank discussion, Wells was willing to pardon Butch. His agreeable personality and pleasant manner won the Utah official to his side.

While Wells was willing to consider amnesty, it would only apply in the state of Utah. Butch was wanted in a number of western states, but Governor Wells had an idea. If they could convince the Union Pacific that Cassidy was going straight, the railroad might be willing to drop all pending charges against him, including those in other states. Furthermore, Butch was willing to go to work for the railroads as a sort of roving troubleshooter—protecting the lines from robbery.

A man named Douglas Preston, working in conjunction with the governor, contacted the Union Pacific. The railway was willing to make a deal—and it was more than willing to hire Butch, at an inflated rate, to police the rail lines. While he was waiting for the final meeting, Butch stayed straight as a token of good faith. He was nervous, though, suspicious that this was a ruse for a carefully planned capture. He requested that the meeting take place near the Green Mountains of Wyoming.

As fate would have it, the train bringing the officials for the meeting was delayed. Butch waited and waited, but Preston and the railroad officials didn't show up at the appointed time. Growing more and more nervous about a double-cross, and more bitter, Butch decided to leave. He had waited nearly a day longer than planned. He left a note: "Damn You! You double-crossed me. I waited all day and you didn't show up. Tell the U.P. to go to hell."

Butch felt he'd gone too far. No one was going to let him go straight. He had tried to become honest, and they wouldn't let him. It was probably at this point that he started to seriously consider going to South America. Unsurprisingly, his next job was against the Union Pacific. Butch supposedly told the Wild Bunch, "I understand that the Union Pacific is looking for trouble. Let's give it to them."

Butch wanted to get revenge and vent his anger against the railroad. It didn't take long to plan the next job. There was a coal station outside of Rawlins, Wyoming, at a place called Tipton where the trains stopped. It was a desolate location, and there were a number of good escape routes. Perhaps the best one was to the Green River region of Utah. Butch presented his plan to his associates, and they agreed it was sound. It was similar to the plan the outlaws had used successfully in the 1899 Wilcox train robbery.

Harvey Logan (a) Harvey Curry, (a) "Kid" Curry, (a) Tom Jones, (a) Bob Jones, se escapó el 27 de Junio de 1903 de la cárcel del Condado de Knox, Knoxville, Tenn., E. U. de A., donde estaba esperando á ser trasladado al presidio de Columbus, Ohio, para cumplir la sentencia de 20 años que se le impuso por circular billetes de bancos alterados, robados del carro del "Great Northern Express" en el ferrocarril "Great Northern," el 3 de Julio de 1901, por asaltadores de caminos de los que Logan era el jefe, y los cuales asaltaron dicho tren, contuvieron con armas de fuego á los empleados del tren, saltaron con dinamita la caja de hierro y sacaron de la misma $45,000 en billetes de banco sin firmar, que se llevaron.

SEÑAS PERSONALES.

NOMBRE..Harvey Logan
ALIAS......Harvey Curry, "Kid" Curry, Bob Jones, Tom Jones, Bob Nevilles, Robt. Nelson, R. T. Whelan.
RESIDENCIA......Se huyó de la cárcel del Condado, Knoxville, Tenn., el sábado 27 de Junio de 1903.
LUGAR DONDE NACIÓ........Dodson, Mo...COLOR...blanco
OCUPACIÓN...Vaquero, tratante
OCUPACIÓN CRIMINAL............Asaltador de bancos y trenes, ladrón de caballos y ganado asaltador de caminos y asesino.
EDAD..38 años [en 1903.]
OJOS OSCUROS...Estatura, 5 pies 7½ pulgadas
PESO ....de 145 á 150 libras. ....CONSTITUCIÓN................Regular
TEZ......... ....trigueña, atezada....................NARIZ......Prominente, larga, grande y recta
COLOR DEL PELO..Negro
BARBA.........afeitada cuando se escapó, pero puede dejarse crecer una barba espesa y bigote de color algo mas claro que el pelo.

ADVERTENCIAS.—Tiene una herida de bala en el brazo derecho, entre la muñeca y el codo; habla despacio; es un poco estevado y de carácter reservado Padece bronquitis aguda, jadea mucho; su estado físico no es del mejor; tiene dos cicatrices en la espalda que parecen proceder de una descarga con perdigones; tiene el hombro izquierdo mucho más bajo que el derecho, á causa de la herida; tiene los brazos más largos que la generalidad de las personas de su estatura; tiene los dedos bastante largos. HARVEY LOGAN también asesinó á Pike Landusky, en Landusky, Montana, el 25 de Diciembre de 1894, y tomó parte en gran número de asaltos y robos, entre ellos el robo del tren del Ferrocarril Unión del Pacífico, en Wilcox, Wyoming, el 2 de Junio de 1899, después de lo cual la fuerza civil alcanzó á Logan y su banda cerca de Casper, Wyoming, y al tratar de prender á los ladrones, el alguacil mayor, Joseph Hazen, del Condado de Converse, Wyoming fué asesinado.

HARVEY LOGAN.
Retrato tomado en 1900.

NOMBRE......................George Parker
ALIAS........."Butch" Cassidy [a] George Cassidy; [a] Ingerfield.
NACIONALIDAD ....Americano
OCUPACIÓN............Vaquero, tratante
OCUPACIÓN CRIMINAL......Ladrón de bancos y asaltador de caminos, ladrón de ganado y caballos.
EDAD..................36 años [en 1901]
ESTATURA..............5 pies 9 pulgadas
PESO...165
CONSTITUCIÓN................Regular
TEZ...Clara
COLOR DEL PELO................Blondo
OJOS...................................Azules
BIGOTE...............Leonado, si lo usa
OBSERVACIONES.—Tiene dos cicatrices en la nuca; cicatriz pequeña debajo del ojo izquierdo, pequeño lunar en la pantorrilla. "Butch" Cassidy es conocido como un criminal principalmente en Wyoming, Utah, Idaho, Colorado y Nevada, y ha cumplido sentencia en el presidio del Estado de Wyoming en Laramie por robo, pero

GEORGE PARKER.
432 B

GEORGE PARKER.
469 R
Último retrato tomado el 21 de Noviembre de

When Butch Cassidy fled to South America, the Pinkertons printed Wanted posters in Spanish.

Pinkerton Archives

The Wild Bunch rode several hundred miles to get into position. Along the way, they left extra horses at key locations and fine-tuned their getaway plans. On the last day, the outlaws walked their horses to the coal station to save their strength. They fed and watered the mounts against the hard ride to follow. It was August 29, 1900.

When the train arrived at about two in the morning, Butch and Kid Curry jumped on board. At gunpoint they made the express man uncouple the train. They blew up and looted the safe, and got away with around fifty thousand dollars. This was an expensive bit of revenge.

Butch was on a roll. The Pinkertons, not to mention every lawman in the West, were on high alert, looking for Butch and his gang. But he knew he'd need a little more money before he could slip out of the country, so he planned to hit the bank in Winnemucca, Nevada, right on the heels of this job. This was going to be his last haul.

On September 19, 1900, Butch Cassidy and the Wild Bunch robbed the Nevada bank. An outlaw named Will Carver had slipped into the lobby first, dressed like a hobo with a shabby bedroll. No one suspected that concealed in the bedding was a new Winchester—cocked and loaded. The holdup went off as planned, and the gang rode off with a cool thirty-two thousand dollars. The outlaws made their way to Texas for one last big Wild Bunch party at their favorite house of ill repute, Hell's Half Acre, before going their separate ways.

After a short stay in New York, Butch Cassidy, the Sundance Kid, and a woman named Etta Place sailed for South America. There they tried ranching, were guards at a mine, and did a number of outlaw jobs—wearing out their welcome quite quickly. By 1908, word got out that they'd been killed in Bolivia. The outlaws were probably glad to have this rumor spread—indeed, they probably started it.

Most historians now agree that Butch and Sundance came back to the United States sometime between 1910 and 1913 and led separate lives. There are numerous accounts of both Butch and Sundance visiting acquaintances in the United States after this time. Such stories are cloaked in secrecy, since friends and family didn't want their loved ones apprehended. There was still a price on Butch's head, so he had to be careful. But Matt Warner, Elza Lay, and others claimed that Butch visited them during this time.

Butch worked in a number of places, and most likely lived in Spokane, Washington, part of the time. It's thought he took a new name— William Phillips. It is also rumored that he worked at ranching and mining—even as a mercenary. Most agree he spent the later part of his life as a businessman in the Pacific Northwest.

LeRoy Parker, a.k.a. Butch Cassidy, is reported to have died in 1937.

The Castle Gate
—✦— Payroll Robbery —✦—
The Most Technical Robbery Ever Pulled in Utah

The daring and well-planned Castle Gate payroll robbery of 1897 made Butch Cassidy's reputation—on both sides of the law. It was considered a criminal masterpiece, leaving little doubt that Butch Cassidy was one of the greatest criminal strategists the West had ever seen. This job also made him the undisputed leader of the gang known as the Wild Bunch.

Large, rich veins of coal had made Pine Canyon in Carbon County, Utah, an important mining center. The Castle Gate Mine, owned by the Pleasant Valley Coal Company, was the largest mining concern in the area, employing hundreds of men.

It also had a tempting payroll. It didn't take long for such a prize to catch the attention of the Wild Bunch. And the mine, near Price, Utah, was between two famous hideouts—Brown's Hole and Robber's Roost—making a disappearing act after a heist easier.

The Denver and Rio Grande Railroad and the Pleasant Valley Coal Company were understandably nervous about the amount of outlaw activity in the area. To thwart robberies, the payroll trains were well guarded and paydays and routines were constantly changed. Miners never knew on which day they'd be paid. Even the mine's paymaster didn't always know when the money was due to arrive from Salt Lake City.

Butch had carefully studied the scenario and decided that a direct attack on the train would be too risky. He concluded that the best approach would be to rob the paymaster just after he took the money from the train. Since no one knew when the money would show up, the outlaws had to be ready, waiting about inconspicuously until the payroll came in.

The sky was robin's-egg blue and the April sun promised a warm afternoon. E. L. Carpenter, paymaster for the Pleasant Valley Coal Company, had a sore toe, so he hadn't changed out of his bedroom slippers before picking up the payroll from the noon train. He could hear the whistle blast signaling to the miners that later that day they would be paid. Paydays always made him nervous, and he'd be happy when this one was over.

As Carpenter gingerly lifted his sore foot onto the wooden stairs leading up to his office, he caught the subtle glint of light on the barrel of a well-used Colt. He felt the powerful prod of the .45 in his ribs as the man came in close. In a quiet voice, the smiling cowboy with the big gun said in his right ear, "I'll take them money bags, sir. Stay calm since I'd hate to shoot a hole in you."

Butch Cassidy had caught Carpenter by complete surprise. It seemed impossible to Carpenter that he was being robbed while hundreds of miners milled about, waiting for their pay. But most of the men were foreigners who didn't speak much English. They probably had no idea what was going on. And there was no mistaking that six-gun. Without a fight, he loosened his fingers on the large case and the money sacks. Carpenter's assistant, a man named Lewis, threw down the bag of silver he was carrying and prudently dove into the hardware store when he saw the gun.

Now that he thought of it, Carpenter realized he'd seen this cowboy and one other sitting on the stairs when he'd walked out to the train. In fact, they'd been hanging about for days. He noticed the two unsaddled horses the men rode. They were tied next to his office. One of the men had now mounted and had his hand on his pistol.

Horses were rare in this mining town—that should have been a clue.

The canyon was so steep and narrow that there was barely enough room for the train and the buildings that served the miners. It was nearly impossible to bring in a wagon. Saddle horses were discouraged. Besides, the miners weren't stockmen—few, if any, had mounts at all.

Butch quietly walked to the man on the horse, Elza Lay, and handed him some of the loot. As Butch grabbed the reins of his horse, Carpenter regained some of his lost courage and ran, sore foot and all, up the stairs to his office yelling, "Robbers! Robbers!"

Someone fired a rifle.

The loitering miners pushed in closer to see what was going on. Butch's well-trained horse became nervous. When Butch tossed up a money bag near his horse's head, the animal spooked and bolted down the street.

For a moment, Butch looked after his mount. There he was, alone, horseless, stunned, gun holstered, a large bag of Castle Gate gold in one hand. He ran for his frightened mount. Quick-thinking Elza headed off the mare. After several futile tries, he grabbed the reins and brought the gray, named Babe, back to his partner. Butch snatched the reins and, in one jump, managed to get seated on the tall horse while still carrying the gold. Babe reared up several times. Elza spurred his horse, and Babe followed him down the narrow way.

Beyond a section house up the canyon, the robbers stopped and quickly put the money into canvas bags, making transport easier. They had at least seven thousand dollars in twenty-dollar gold pieces, some currency, and silver. They left the silver, which was too heavy to carry, and picked up the saddles they'd hidden.

Since there were few horses in the canyon, the outlaws had pretended to be training their "racehorses"—working them on the steep canyon trails. In that era, it was the custom for racing buffs to condition their animals by riding cross-country without a saddle. Each day after working out their mounts, Butch and Elza hung around the saloon, drinking and loafing. They'd become temporary fixtures at the watering hole, so they hadn't looked out of place in a town with few horses.

Carpenter ran for the telegraph office. The nearest law was in Price, 10 miles away. The telegraph man looked up at the frustrated Carpenter and told him the lines had been cut. Thinking clearly, Carpenter hobbled to the train in his bedroom slippers and told the engineer to fire up the engine. There was still a head of steam, so off they went. Carpenter didn't know it, but he passed Butch and Elza, who were behind the section house saddling up.

The train screamed toward Price.

Carpenter had the whistle pulled down, signaling to the town that something was wrong. When the train pulled to a stop, Sheriff Donant was at the platform. Donant wasn't thinking as clearly as Carpenter. It took him several hours to get his posse organized—and then he took off in the wrong direction. In the meantime, Carpenter telegraphed the news about the robbery to all the local towns.

But the third member of the outlaw gang, Joe Walker, had cut the telegraph wires out of the canyon. He was leaving Price when he saw the train come in, whistle blowing. Joe knew the law would be on their trail soon. He'd planned on cutting the line to Emery County, west of Price, but decided he'd better meet up with his partners instead.

They rendezvoused at Desert Lake. Butch and Elza decided to lead the posse on a round-about route while Joe took the money to Florence Creek and back to the hideout in the Roost. Butch knew where he was going, and he wouldn't have the loot to slow him down. Joe would slip off unseen, and no one would be the wiser.

At the same time, posses were gathering in Castle Dale, Huntington, and Cleveland. Some members of the posse were less than enthusiastic about catching up with the robbers. The leader of the Huntington posse, for example, had loaned his horse, Babe, to Butch for this caper and he had no intentions of catching up with his friend.

Butch knew the Utah backcountry like the sun wrinkles on his face. He had mounts and provisions stashed so he could replenish his supplies. He had spent the winter planning this job and had the contingencies covered. Besides, the locals were more than eager to loan or sell a horse. He'd always treated ranchers and farmers with respect—and paid them well for their services. There was little love lost between the local folks and the mining company. At one ranch, Butch and Elza pulled in about midnight with exhausted mounts. Butch asked if they could exchange their exhausted horses for new horses. Butch picked out two good horses and asked the rancher what price was fair. The rancher said twenty dollars. Butch gave him fifty, generating goodwill among the locals and inspiring a lack of cooperation with the law.

It was a long chase, but Butch and Elza were always in control. In the end, the famous lawman Joe Bush was not far behind. The Bush posse was small but dedicated. It also included Carpenter, who was still wearing his bedroom slippers. He was a determined company man.

In Mexican Hat, a black dog named Sunday had befriended Butch and followed him down the trail. The outlaws were traveling fast, and the black dog was keeping up pretty well. However, after a while it began to lag behind. Looking through his field glasses, Butch noted that the Bush posse had pulled ahead of the faithful canine. In fact they'd passed the dog not knowing it was there. Butch could see his furry friend, tongue out, tired, trying to keep up. Butch had a soft spot for animals, especially a dog this faithful. He had Elza wait in the rocks and fire shots at the posse with his Winchester, pinning them down.

Elza knew he wasn't to hit any of the lawmen. Butch's orders were to shoot but never to kill unless there was no other choice. With his long gun, Elza started lobbing shots at the lawmen, who quickly took cover while Butch slipped around them and rescued the faithful hound. He gave the animal a drink, dropped down the draw, and circled ahead of the posse carrying Sunday on his saddle.

"This dog has stayed with me better than most posses," he said. "I've got to respect that."

Dog and outlaws made it to the Flat Tops and lost themselves in the Roost. Butch had planned well. Along the way, they had horses and supplies—and help from other gang members or ranchers as needed. They had ridden south of Price, west to Cleveland, down Buckhorn Wash to San Rafael, across 70 miles of desert.

They met up with Joe Walker and divided up the gold. The posse gave up. No one is sure what happed to the dog, Sunday, but it is certain Butch found a good home for him.

As a postscript to this caper: The outlaws holed up for nearly three months. Legend has it there were a couple of women hanging about camp to make life a little more interesting. The boys played poker until they went stir crazy. About the end of June, the Wild Bunch decided to head back to Brown's Hole where the action was. They rode hard for five days, crossing the Green River and the Book Cliff Mountains and finally hitting Crouse Creek and friendly faces.

They were loaded from the robbery, so they gathered up some party-starved cowboys (at least eight Wild Bunch riders and anyone else who wanted free drinks) and headed over the state line into Carbon County, Wyoming. Their favorite watering holes were in a couple of one-horse towns, Dixon and Baggs. They came into town with guns blazing.

Local merchants started sharpening pencils—this would be good business. Hopefully no one would accidentally get shot. The Bunch all bought new suits, took baths, and got shaves. Some bought new derby hats. Then they started to party.

To say they shot up the towns would be an understatement. In one saloon alone, there were more than twenty-five bullet holes in the bar (who knows about the roof) before the party ended. It was all in fun—and no innocent bystanders got killed—although one imagines most sensible townsfolk, accustomed to these occasional group forays with the bottle, sent all the respectable women and children to the country. Every bullet hole was gladly paid for (a dollar a hole). Dixon and Baggs had quite a reputation for hosting outlaws. Legend has it that a rustler got sick and needed a doctor from the larger town of Rock Springs. No doctor, however, would risk coming. The lofty sum of two thousand dollars in gold was offered, but the good physician refused to go to the sick man. Lucky for him, he was not taken at gunpoint.

There was a lot of big talk about how well the job had gone, and the money flowed as fast as the whiskey. Rumor has it that Carpenter was the butt of many a toasted glass. One Bunch cowboy even offered to send him a pair of boots since he'd heard that Carpenter was riding with the posse in his bedroom slippers.

The Wild Bunch
The Most Successful Gang of Thieves in the West

No one is exactly sure who coined the name the Wild Bunch. The term probably came around 1895 or 1896 from the good folks in the small Wyoming towns of Baggs and Dixon, just north of the Colorado border.

These two municipalities each vied for the outlaw's dollar. They were conveniently located a few miles apart—just enough distance to give a drinking man with a snoot full a little time to sober up between establishments (presupposing he didn't fall off his horse and wind up in the ditch). Both had a reputation for welcoming a rough crowd. As long as you didn't commit a crime within city limits or harm one of the citizens, what you happened to do somewhere else was your business. No one cared if you were wanted . . . relax and have a few drinks. No one checked Wanted posters here. Outlaws could spend their money freely in relative comfort and safety.

Times were tough. The big trail herds and the thirsty cowboys that accompanied them were long gone. Each town with its accompanying watering holes welcomed hard cash, never mind where it came from. Honest cowhands blowing off steam were certainly welcome, but a regular cowboy didn't have the same disposable income as a certain group coming up from Brown's Hole. These boys would really "cut the wolf loose," as the saying went. They hit the town for days, sometimes weeks. As they rode into town, the locals would say, "Here comes that wild bunch."

The Wild Bunch (a.k.a. The Hole-in-the-Wall Gang) Left to right: Harry Longabaugh (the Sundance Kid), Will Carver (Will Case), Ben Kilpatrick (the Tall Texan), Harvey Logan (Kid Curry), and Robert LeRoy Parker (Butch Cassidy)
Denver Public Library, Western History Collection, photo taken in Fort Worth, Texas

The name stuck.

When they were in town, there was always a big party. Whiskey and beer flowed like spring water; friendly bullets of excitement peppered the roof, punctuated the floor, and accented the bar. Ladies of the evening worked double or triple shifts. Games of chance started up and never stopped. The outlaws bought new clothes and stocked up on extras at the dry goods store. They paid the livery handsomely for horse care. Some bought new saddles with all the trimmings. New weapons and ammunition were purchased at the hardware store or gun shop. An establishment might do a month's worth of business in one day. The outlaws paid appreciatively for home-cooked meals, while the residents listened attentively to tales and adventures.

Sure they tore up the town, but they paid for (in gold) damages two or three times what something was worth. The Wild Bunch left few debts. After the bender was over, the outlaws would be nearly broke, nursing savage headaches. They'd head to their hideout to cool off and plan another crime. The local merchants, in the meantime, would be smiling as they did a final tally in their ledgers, stuffing away the extra gold coins for rainy days.

It was important to have a safe place to drink and blow off steam. There was also something to be said for partying in a secure setting and as a group. Most of the time the Bunch were careful men. Occasionally, they let their guard down when drinking, as Wilbur "Bub" Meeks found out. Bub got a little restless at one Baggs-Dixon party and rode up to Fort Bridger for a change of pace. He was loaded after a recent robbery.

He had a fancy saddle and bridle and gold that was burning a hole in his front pocket. In retrospect he should have stayed with the boys he knew, but how do you know when it's your turn to be unlucky? While he was tilting his elbow in Bridger, the local post office got robbed. Bub probably wasn't involved. There was little more than one hundred dollars in the take. Nevertheless, he was a suspected outlaw, and he had plenty of money and a fancy new outfit—all damning evidence.

The locals easily got the drop on the man, his wits dulled by too much firewater, and tied him up while a civic-minded gent rode to Evanston for a real lawman. While Bub was waiting for the law, he was rumored to have downed a number of bottles of Old Crow (which didn't do much for his thinking). He wasn't going to take getting arrested lightly—he was going to get really drunk. He was hauled off to Evanston and a real jail. Deputy Sheriff Bob Calverly had a bright idea. Bub was a known member of the Bunch, so Calverly naturally suspected his involvement in the robbery that had taken place in Montpelier, Idaho. A teller was brought in from the bank and identified the unlucky Bub as one of the Wild Bunch bandits.

Bub had two good lawyers, handsomely paid for by Butch and the gang. So what if they had to do another job to get the funds? Bub Meeks was a pard. He was liked, and the Wild Bunch did what they could for a colleague. The defense did their best, but Bub didn't have a chance. He was convicted and sentenced to thirty-two years in the Idaho State Prison. He knew the Bunch had done all they could. After all, he had the best lawyers stolen money could buy, but the jury was against him from the start.

Bub hated prison life and longed to be back on his horse in Brown's Hole or riding the outlaw trail. He vowed to do what it took to get out of the pen. Each day he ate a bit of soap when he was in the washroom. It tasted awful, but he knew from previous discussions around the campfire that, if he were lucky, he might look like he had a case of tuberculosis. The trick worked and he played it for all he was worth. He'd also quit eating so he'd lose weight, and he faked a bad cough. He practiced spitting up a yellow, bubbly phlegm. Meeks was put into the prison hospital. The medical opinion: He did have TB. The ruse had worked.

A contractor was making repairs on the prison walls, and a frame was erected near Bub's window—a window that he could get out of. Any risk was worth taking to avoid life in prison. He could get out, but not down. It was almost a two-story jump, but what the heck. Bub felt that it was worth it. He longed for mountain air, and he'd die if he had to stay in prison. He crawled out the window onto the scaffold and sucked up his courage. He was ready to take that big leap in the name of freedom. Bub shut his eyes, hoped for the best, and jumped. He hit the ground, but things didn't turn out as well as he'd planned. He fell very hard, and in addition to other injuries, he fractured one leg. Bone poked out of the flesh in several places. The prison doctors had no choice but to cut off the limb to save his life.

In an ironic way, his trick worked. A one-legged man couldn't ride with the outlaws, and it wasn't cost-effective to keep him in prison for another thirty-two years. After a long convalescence, one-legged Bub was cut loose. He made his way back to Brown's Hole, but there'd be no more outlawing for him.

The term *wild bunch* has been used rather loosely in the West. Any group of wild and rowdy men could merit this handle. Indeed, several gangs of outlaws in Texas, Kansas, and Oklahoma were called the Wild Bunch. However, the sobriquet as we know it today stuck to the group that frequented the Rocky Mountains area. At one time Butch Cassidy tried to rename this loose collection of men the Train Robbers Syndicate, but the name never caught on. By then, even the press was calling the outlaws the Wild Bunch. The name had a certain western charm and romance attached to it. And the group did earn its name.

Contrary to newspaper accounts, the Wild Bunch wasn't a tightly organized band of outlaws. It was a professional association, a common-wealth of men who worked together now and then around a central core. Butch Cassidy is thought of as the leader, and for the most part he was, but there were others, notably the Sundance Kid, Elza Lay, and Kid Curry.

Some historians have suggested that more than one hundred men might have graced the Wild Bunch ranks over the years. A more accu-rate count might be thirty or forty men who were considered card-carrying members. Out of this group, a handful formed the core. The others came and went as it suited them. The Wild Bunch didn't do crimes in large groups. It was rare for more than eight men to go into the field at once. Most of the jobs were carefully planned, and a large group wasn't needed.

A lot of friends and cowboys would ride with the outlaws on party runs or on a little midnight rustling, but they couldn't really be considered professional outlaws. Perhaps their presence is why the number has been so enlarged.

It is also logical to assume that while the reputation of the Wild Bunch spread, a number of crimes that they didn't commit were blamed on them. The outlaws made good copy, the stuff of folk legends and dime novels—and increased newspaper sales. The legend and the accompanying misinformation that trailed them grew as fast as the presses could print. In some accounts they were Robin Hoods of the West, with fast six-guns and led by the good-looking, charismatic, misunderstood Butch Cassidy, the "Robber King." For better or worse, the gang members were sometimes portrayed as bad guys with "hearts of gold." They robbed the oppressive rich, railroads, and banks; they were generous with their ill-gotten booty, helping the poor; they treated the locals with respect. They weren't bloody criminals; they didn't make a practice of shooting people.

The bankers and the railroad moguls, however, weren't laughing.

Butch Cassidy was easygoing, he liked people, and he wasn't mean spirited. The Wild Bunch reflected his personality. Compared to the Black Jack Ketchum Gang, which operated about the same time and in the same territory, the Wild Bunch was pretty gentle. "Black Jack" Ketchum and crew left bodies in the wake of their crimes (between twelve and twenty depending on whom you want to believe). Black Jack (whose first name was really Tom) was a brutal, no-nonsense killer who was happy to shoot if it pleased him—and it often did. He was hard, but he was successful at his trade. (Before he swung, he had stolen more than $250,000, a tidy sum in that day.) Surprisingly, some of the Wild Bunch rode with the Ketchum Gang during their own gang's long hiatuses. (Butch liked to take time to party and carefully plan more crimes.) Elza Lay, for example, rode with Black Jack on his last robbery—one of the big mistakes of his life. (The job turned sour and two sheriffs were killed.) Some of Ketchum's gang also rode with, and later joined, the Wild Bunch.

Will Case (a.k.a. William R. Carver) rode for both gangs, but he had a falling out with Black Jack and became a full-time Wild Buncher. He was about five foot six or seven, with sandy blond hair and a ruddy complexion. The *San Angelo Standard* suggested that he was unassuming and quiet, that he was retiring, and that he disliked publicity and kept to himself. He enjoyed a well-planned job and felt comfortable with Butch. Will enjoyed the quietness of the desert and solitude of the plains. He avoided society when he could. He wasn't as well known as some of the other members of the gang, but he did help with a few robberies. In 1912 he took a fatal bullet while robbing a train.

Another transfer from the Ketchum Gang was the "Tall Texan," Ben Kilpatrick. He was well liked and soft spoken but no one to mess around with. He could hold his own. He was considered quite a lady's man among the Bunch—which is saying something. He was a little over 6 feet tall, 185 pounds, and had light brown eyes and dark hair. He was born in West Texas in 1874. Before associating with the Wild Bunch, the Tall Texan had been a member of Black Jack Ketchum's band, with whom he cut his eye teeth as a train bandit. He eventually had a falling out with Ketchum and left the gang. He was good friends with Carver and Kid Curry.

Unlike Black Jack's gang, the Wild Bunch leadership wasn't dictatorial. Members were free to come and go as they pleased. Jobs were planned and members participated as they saw fit. Since Butch and his first lieutenant (and best friend), Elza Lay, were so successful, there was never any shortage of outlaws wanting in on the action. Never in the history of the Old West was a benevolent crime boss so successful in his criminal planning.

In 1899, after that fateful caper with Black Jack, Elza was arrested in Eddy County, New Mexico, and sent to prison for life. (He was released in 1906 for good behavior.) Once Elza was out of the loop, the Sundance Kid became Butch's right-hand man and chief lieutenant for the Wild Bunch. Butch and Sundance were very good friends and had a working respect, but Sundance wasn't as close to Butch as Elza had been.

Ben Kilpatrick, a.k.a. the Tall Texan
Pinkerton Archives

The philosophy of the Wild Bunch was similar to a Native American warrior society, which is one of the reasons for its success. The men were a group of independent warrior-outlaws, who came together on a project if it suited them. There was no compulsory drafting of men into projects, no strong-arm techniques. You worked if it suited you and you liked the job. After a raid, it wasn't uncommon for the group to split up and go their separate ways, maybe returning, maybe not. In the winter, when the jobs were fewer, many members of the Wild Bunch left Brown's Hole for Robber's Roost, which was considered the outlaws' winter resort. An outlaw could come and go as he pleased. He could plan his own job, taking any gang member who wanted to go. If you agreed to a raid that Butch Cassidy planned, you did things his way. With his successful record, you were generally happy to follow orders.

Most of the members of the Wild Bunch came from humble, hardworking stock. The Robin Hood newspaper hype had its roots in reality, even if it was sometimes exaggerated. The working man, the family man, was respected and protected. Many of the outlaws had seen firsthand what the giant ranching concerns and the railroads could do to the family farm or ranch. Others had seen bank foreclosures and the looks on the faces of the homeless. Many of the outlaws wanted to go straight, but they felt they were pushed into a life of crime and now had little recourse. This was the day of robber barons, and the West had its share who were driven by power and greed. Many newspaper readers took pleasure in reading about a bank or a train being robbed.

Butch Cassidy tried to be nonviolent. Butch was proud to say, "I haven't killed anyone." It was also known that he gave strict orders to his gang never to shoot to kill—unless there was no other choice. He expected his outlaws to be crack shots, but never to kill posse members who were chasing them. Rather, outlaws were instructed to shoot at the horses. Besides not wanting to waste lives, Butch also knew that if his gang killed a lawman in the line of duty, it would sooner or later turn public opinion against them. And if they were caught, the punishment would be severe. These men had families.

Nevertheless, the Wild Bunch members were still criminals. They held up people at gunpoint and took what didn't belong to them.

According to reports, Kid Curry was one of the few bloodthirsty men in the Wild Bunch. He also had the largest price on his head. For a time he was more infamous than Butch Cassidy. He probably wasn't completely sane, but Butch could control him. In 1897 there was a reported power play between the two for leadership of the Bunch, but Butch proved to be a superior planner, and Curry was eventually smart enough to realize it. Besides, every job he had planned on his own had nearly cost him his freedom and netted almost nothing. Later on, toward the end of his outlaw career, he pulled a successful job or two, but by then he had seen masters at work.

With the exception of Kid Curry, who tended to enjoy killing, the Bunch generally trusted fast horses and good getaway plans over gunfire. Unlike many bands of outlaws in the West that tended to operate haphazardly, the Wild Bunch had exceptional leadership. Few criminal organizations planned better or were more successful during their heyday. Here is a short list of the gang's major crimes:

April 1897	Butch Cassidy, Elza Lay, and Joe Walker rob the Pleasant Valley Coal Company at Castle Gate, Utah.
June 1897	Kid Curry, Sundance Kid, Tom O'Day, and Walt Punteney rob the Butte County Bank in Belle Fourche, South Dakota.
April 1899	Sundance Kid, Kid Curry, and George Curry rob the Club Saloon in Elko, Nevada.
June 1899	Kid Curry, George Curry, and Sundance Kid rob the Union Pacific train in Wilcox, Wyoming.
July 1899	Elza Lay, Sam Ketchum, and Will Carver rob the Colorado Southern train in Folsom, New Mexico.
August 1900	Butch Cassidy, Sundance Kid, and Kid Curry rob a train at Tipton, Wyoming.
September 1900	Butch Cassidy, Sundance Kid, Ben Kilpatrick, Kid Curry, and Will Carver rob the Winnemucca Bank in Winnemucca, Nevada.
July 1901	Kid Curry, Ben Kilpatrick, and Camilla Hanks rob the Great Northern train in Wagner, Montana.

Strictly speaking, the Wild Bunch existed for about five years—from 1896 to 1901. However, since many of the core outlaws were good friends and worked together before and after this five-year period, a student of western history will often see the name Wild Bunch associated with crimes before or after these dates.

However the dates are crunched, the Wild Bunch enjoyed a robbing spree with little interruption. They were one of the most successful bands of criminals in the West during their heyday. At one time, the railroad nearly bought off Butch and his crew, giving them pardons for past crimes. When they factored in the cost of future losses and the price of law enforcement, railroad officials felt this tactic would be cheaper than fighting the Wild Bunch.

Even experienced outlaws have bad days, though. On June 2, 1899, near Wilcox, Wyoming, the Bunch flagged down the Union Pacific's Overland Limited using a warning lantern. The boys got the express car loose and blasted their way into the locked car with TNT. The Expressman, E. C. Woodcock, had stubbornly refused to open the car door. He survived the savage blast but was blown the length of the car. The safe with the money was still intact, too. However, a large consignment of raspberries was blown to bits, making a sticky mess.

Legend says there was some debate on how much dynamite to use to blow off the door of the safe. The first barrage of TNT had literally blown the car to pieces, but it hadn't done more than ruin the paint on the heavy safe. With a bit more TNT for good measure, Butch blasted the safe so they could get at the cash. As shown in the movie *Butch Cassidy and the Sundance Kid*, money was blown over the land. In the movie, Robert Redford's character, the Sundance Kid, says, "Think you've used enough dynamite, there, Butch."

Apparently, it was a funny sight, and those who saw it never forgot the irony of the situation. One of the wildest, roughest, most successful band of robbers the West had ever seen was scrambling about like eager chickens trying to pluck up the bills blown over the landscape. (One can't help thinking that as soon as the outlaws rode away, the place was probably overrun with passengers doing the same thing.) Apparently, the scramble for money wasn't too dignified, but the last laugh was on the railroad, since the gang rode away with more than thirty-four thousand dollars and some jewelry.

As time went by, making a clean getaway became more and more difficult. The law had become "too acquainted" with how the Wild Bunch did business, according to Butch. He had long argued to his inner circle that they needed a serious change of scenery—the odds of getting shot or captured were getting shorter and shorter, and there had been too many close calls. Butch was a good poker player—he knew when to fold his cards.

He planned to head to South America. There, an outlaw could start fresh. South America, Argentina in particular, was on the verge of an economic boom that appealed to aspiring bandits from the States with a heavy price on their heads. Butch invited some of his Bunch friends to go with him. Obviously, Sundance was interested. Kid Curry had a passing interest in going but decided to stay in the States. Apparently travel didn't appeal to the others, so they decided to stay as well. They must not have felt the increasing threat that Butch and Sundance did.

Butch and Sundance needed one more score to get the additional funds they needed to escape in style, so they risked one more job. That score was the Winnemucca National Bank in Winnemucca, Nevada. The take was $32,640.

On November 21, 1900, they had one last farewell Wild Bunch party in the red-light districts of Texas. They stayed at Fannie Porter's luxurious four-star brothel. Some members of the gang—the Sundance Kid, the Tall Texan, Butch Cassidy, Will Case, and Kid Curry—had a picture taken at the John Swartz Studio, which would prove to be an imprudent move. Butch sent the picture to some folks in Winnemucca with his compliments. The photo quickly fell into the hands of the Pinkertons and lawmen. It gave the trackers something tangible to work with—faces to plaster on Wanted posters. (It is the only Wild Bunch picture in existence.)

Butch and Sundance left for South America in February 1901. The rest of the gang went their separate ways. Without Butch's direction, most of the remaining Bunchers were killed or jailed.

Following are some highlights of some of the core members of the Wild Bunch. Most were in their early thirties when they rode the outlaw trail. Many had been pretty fair stockmen or cowboys at one time. Nearly all were expert horsemen and crack shots.

- Wilbur "Bub" Meeks (sometimes called Bob) was a likable man. Good natured and a bit quiet, he was a fine cowboy and an excellent rustler and horseman from Fremont County, Wyoming. After he started making that fine outlaw money, he got a little flashy—both with his clothes and his tact. This would be his downfall. In prison he jumped two stories while attempting to escape. He lost his leg as a result and was released. He then went straight. His Mormon family had migrated to Wyoming in the 1880s and settled into the Big Horn basin. Joe Meeks, who also rubbed shoulders with the gang, was his cousin.

- Will Case (Billy, Bill, William R. Carver) had a quick draw. A one-time member of Black Jack Ketchum's gang in the Southwest, he was a good friend of Kid Curry and a companion of Lillie Davis. Just before the Winnemucca bank robbery, Will had an altercation with a very large skunk on the outskirts of town and took a direct hit; during the robbery, his odor was enough to knock out the folks in the bank. He didn't dress well and never looked like a cowboy or a westerner; he liked to wear a beat-up, off-the-rack suit, heavy boots, and a derby hat. He was good natured but could turn mean when drinking. He loved apricot brandy. He was shot in Sonora, Texas, by Sheriff Briant on April 2, 1901.

- Flat Nose Curry (George Curry) was born in 1871 in Prince Edward Island, Canada. A skilled rustler, he spent a lot of time in Utah but committed very few crimes in the state—the worst was stealing a milk cow. He was called Flat Nose for good reason—it was said he got kicked in the face by a cow or a horse and his face was rather flat. He was nearly caught by Sheriffs Jesse Tyler and William Preece near Moab, Utah. He was shot near Green River, Utah, by a relentless Preece and later died of blood poisoning from that wound. A gang leader in his own right, leading robberies in the Powder River area of Wyoming, he was a card-carrying member of the Hole-in-the-Wall Gang. Legend has it that after he died, a tobacco pouch was made from his skin while the rest of his body was placed in a barrel of alcohol and pickled until 1950.

- The Tall Texan (Ben Kilpatrick) was a good-looking, cheerful man who liked to play jokes on the other members of the gang. Fast with a gun, he had been born into an outlaw family that specialized in rustling in Texas. He couldn't read and was embarrassed by his illiteracy, so he always ordered beans and ham in restaurants—pretending he could read the menu. After the Wagner, Montana, job, Ben took his money and headed east with Della Rose (Laura Bullion) for an extended party. He was captured and did a stretch in prison. After his release, he and another con held up a train on March 12, 1912; he was shot and killed by a Wells Fargo man during the robbery.

- Wat the Watcher (Walter Punteney) was a fine cowhand and horseman, good with machines, and a crack shot. He was often the man who cased towns before a job. He lived until the 1950s. He always claimed that Butch and Sundance were not murderers.

- Tom O'Day (sometimes called Peep) was a minor gang member. A lookout, he often held the horses during a job. He was addicted to playing poker—it is said he sat in the same chair for two full days playing stud. He was also good with explosives and blew a few safes. Tom was a good-natured lad and a practical joker. He was with Sundance and Kid Curry at the ill-fated Belle Fourche robbery in South Dakota. He never made it back to the Bunch after that; he was flushed out of hiding by a man hunting rabbits and accidentally ran into the posse hunting him. Later he got caught stealing a herd of saddle horses and was jailed. After being released, he went to Texas, where he was promptly shot.

- Harry Tracy killed a man and drifted up to Brown's Hole, where he met Butch and Sundance. He was quite a pistol shot—accurate even from the back of a galloping horse. In Wyoming in 1902, he was surrounded by vigilantes; the prospects looked hopeless. Rather than give up, he put his faithful Colt to his head and sent himself to his next reward (or lack of reward).

- Deaf Charlie (Camilla Hanks) was deaf in one ear. He was born in DeWitt County, Texas, in 1863 and he was a good cowboy. He was arrested in 1892 for train robbery in Teton County, Montana, and did a stretch in prison. At age thirty-eight he was released and quickly jumped back into the outlaw game—taking a hand in the Great Northern Railway robbery at Wagner, Montana. A while later, he drifted around Texas and got into a barroom fight in San Antonio on April 17, 1902. When the law showed up, he went for his gun but was too slow and was killed.

- William Cruzan (Bill) was a blue-ribbon rustler; his specialty was horses. He knew the backcountry better than any man alive, one of his friends remarked.

- Jess Linsley at one time worked for the railroad and had a good knowledge of trains and their operation. He must have lost a few fights since he was missing most of his front teeth.

- Jim Lowe was a dandy; he was careful about combing his hair and always wore a tie and a pin. He was a small man and at one time a barkeeper.

- Tom McCarty was a sometime associate of the Wild Bunch—especially in the early days. Like Butch Cassidy and Matt Warner, he was a Mormon boy (son of a doctor) turned by easy money and good times. He was born in 1855 on a Utah ranch. An occasional family man, he led a life of rustling and robbery. In the early part of his career, being older than his partners, he was the leader of the McCarty Gang. Along with Butch and Matt (his brother-in-law), the gang did a fair share of rustling—until they got greedy and looked for a bigger score. After they robbed the bank in Telluride, Colorado, all three were launched into the big time—with prices on their heads and posses on their trail. (Tom was recognized as they left town, and their cover was blown.) Tom could be a little feisty, although he got along well enough with his friends. He never backed down from a fight and was inclined to shoot first if pushed. He wasn't as fast a draw or as deadly a shot as Matt or Butch, but he was good enough to be considered very dangerous and unpredictable. It was probably Tom who taught Butch his first lessons on planning a crime—and more importantly, how to get away after the crime had been committed. At one time, Tom was married to Matt's sister. He always remained on good terms with his early partners in crime, but as the Wild Bunch rose to prominence, Tom went his own way—although he and Matt still did occasional jobs together. When his relatives were killed in the Delta, Colorado, bank holdup, he started to take a lower profile. Eventually he drifted to the Bitterroot country in Montana and did some ranching. He got into a fight and was shot to death around the turn of the century.

Brown's Hole
A Valley Outside the Law

Brown's Hole: Honest ranchers, outlaws, rustlers, gunmen . . . welcome! Sheriffs, marshals, deputies, busybodies, range detectives, cattle barons . . . enter at your own risk!

Brown's Hole may have been the last no-man's-land in the West. A cowboy there didn't ask a stranger many questions, nor was it wise to ask a man's name unless it was offered. There were more than a few shallow graves without markers—bodies not intended to be found. There were plenty of makeshift headstones, too, marking the final resting places of men such as "Mexican Joe" Herrera, who was supposedly knifed during a volatile game of stud poker. A number of toughs were playing cards at the Crowley place (which still is standing). Mexican Joe had some bad luck, so he started dealing off the bottom of the deck. He didn't leave the table alive. It was a hot game, so he was buried a few feet from the south wall of the cabin so the boys could get back to their game and whiskey. He learned the hard way. Folks in the Hole took their poker seriously, and cheating was a breach of etiquette that could end in a death sentence.

It wasn't until the end of the 1800s that a lawman dared ride into Brown's Hole.

Never mind that Joe Philbrick was wanted in three states. He was handy. Old Joe pinned on a tin star only because he was in a bind. He needed some walking-about money, and he understood the veiled threat of extradition if he didn't play along with the local gendarmes. A lawman riding into the Hole might just as well stick a gun to his forehead or

Hole-in-the-Wall/Brown's Park area
Denver Public Library, Western History Collection, Illustration by Merritt D. Houghton, Laramie, Wyoming

sleep with a mess of rattlesnakes. Local lawmen weren't cowards. They'd face a bad man in the streets with Colt handguns or Winchester rifles. They'd trail a bad guy across the country and back if need be. But if an outlaw managed to slip into Brown's Hole, no God-fearing lawman, especially if he had a family, was eager to follow.

Nearly all the Wild Bunch, including Butch Cassidy and the Sundance Kid, among other notable Utah outlaws, found refuge in this sanctuary. Matt Warner's cabin, like so many others, still stands—although it's weathered and showing its age. No one really knows how many head of rustled cattle ended up making the basin their new home, or how many head of rustled cattle stayed long enough to fatten on the rich valley grass and were re-branded before being driven to market. This was a sanctuary for men on the run, too.

Such men were welcomed—as were their stolen herds. The folks in the Hole had a code that was followed, sort of. No stealing or gunslinging among the residents—permanent or temporary. What you did outside was your business, but in the basin called Brown's Hole you respected personal property and did no gunslinging—unless it was absolutely necessary or you had a good reason for what you were doing. Then, if there was a problem, you solved it yourself with Colts, Winchesters, knives, or fists.

Men on the dodge could buy, trade, or exchange horses with the locals—but they'd better not take a local cow or horse without permission. They might be hunted down and hung. Outlaws were expected to treat the local women with respect, and for the most part they did. Cowboys, ranchers, and outlaws socialized together as equals at the area's many dances, get-togethers, and picnics. Folks in the Hole loved their parties.

As a rule, outlaws and rustlers could always expect a good meal from one of the permanent residents as they passed through. It was common for those on the dodge to get fattened up at a rancher's table—likely on stolen beef. Drawing no pay, they'd help with the chores as a matter of course. Butch Cassidy, Elza Lay, Kid Curry, and the Sundance Kid, among others, hung out at favorite ranches. These men were excellent cowboys and enjoyed lending a hand, especially during roundups. They were known as men who'd pitch in if a chore needed doing. This sort of behavior promoted local goodwill. Most of the ranches had winter and summer ranges—with accompanying line shacks or cabins. It was not uncommon for a man "laying over" after a job to stay at such a place. Naturally, he was expected to ride line and keep his eye on the livestock (which were often as hot as the iron used to change the brand).

Members of the Wild Bunch were especially fond of the Bassett and Crouse ranches, where they ate good meals, read fine books, drank whiskey, talked, planned, and played poker. Charlie Crouse and Butch were fast friends. Charlie wasn't a professional outlaw, but he was a tough character one didn't mess around with—he also liked his whiskey and cards. One time he shot a drifter who stepped over the line of propriety. Crouse buried the man under a conspicuous pile of rocks—which served as a warning that he meant business. He was gruff and crude, but he had a kind streak. His wife was beloved by everyone and a fine cook. Charlie and his wife were dirt poor when they started their ranch. They had a fry pan, a Dutch oven, a bed, a buffalo robe, and a rifle—and a dream to build a comfortable home (which was enjoyed by many an outlaw). It didn't hurt that the Crouse ranch was one of the most isolated spots in the basin. Charlie also had a pretty daughter named Minnie that Butch Cassidy took a fancy to. She was one of his many love interests in the region.

Near the Crouse ranch on August 18, 1896, Butch Cassidy, at least in legend, called a meeting on what is now called Cassidy Point. Supposedly over two hundred outlaws attended the gathering, in what may have been the largest convention of its kind in the West. Butch told his fellow bank robbers, train robbers, cattle thieves, horse thieves, holdup men, highwaymen, and anyone else who cared to listen that what the modern outlaw needed was proper organization. He proposed to call his group the Train Robbers Syndicate. The name never stuck. The term the Wild Bunch seemed more apropos.

Of course, there was a fly in Butch's plan. His friend, Kid Curry, another powerful outlaw, used the forum to try to steal Butch's thunder. Curry naturally offered his services as leader, and there was a division among the rank and file. Rather than shoot it out, Butch good-naturedly proposed a plan that seemed to satisfy and delight those in attendance. Outlaws who wanted to follow Butch were free to do so, while those who wanted to follow Kid Curry should take up with him. In one year they would all meet again at the Point. Whoever had stolen the most money or pulled the most daring job(s) would be the new leader.

Most notably, the Sundance Kid followed Curry. In hindsight, Sundance recognized this was likely a mistake and wished he'd taken up with Butch. The Curry gang pulled the ill-fated, ill-planned Belle Fourche bank job in South Dakota. The gang was eventually caught and jailed—a poor showing for Curry's skills as a leader all the way around.

Butch, on the other hand, along with his close friend Elza Lay, pulled off a number of successful crimes. Elza, who at one time had been looked upon as the informal leader of the Wild Bunch, was probably as careful a strategist as Butch—some say he was the mind in back of Butch Cassidy. Either way, the two of them were a winning combination—unless you were a banker, a railroad man, or a larger rancher. It was during this probationary time that Butch executed the famous Castle Gate payroll robbery. The sheer daring and bravado of this robbery made Butch the undisputed leader of the Wild Bunch.

Brown's Hole regulars, mostly honest folks, often profited handsomely from the ill-gotten booty the temporary residents brought in. Many a Brown's Hole stockman, who would never consider stealing in the regular sense of the word, built up herds of cattle and horses by acquiring questionable livestock at prices considerably below market rate. Some outlaws even became silent partners with various locals, helping with financial support or hooved assets. Furthermore, many outlaws were thought of as lonely "good boys" who'd made a wrong turn (or several dozen wrong turns). Some were informally "adopted" by local settlers, who took the poor miscreants under their respective family wings—turning a blind eye to the criminal activity.

Just as important, those outside the law tended to be careless and generous with their money. They brought hard cash into an area where it was scarce.

Men on the dodge liked having a safe home base. Ranchers were sometimes provided with horses. The understanding was that the outlaw could trade his worn-out stock for fresh animals as needed. He or his band could expect a good meal and a few supplies, too. If the outlaw were in a hurry, a rancher might discover worn-out ponies in the corral the next morning. Many outlaws, Butch and Sundance, for example, had small outfits of their own. Matt Warner had the beginnings of a very nice working horse ranch. He had hands to look after his outfit while he was out raiding.

For an outlaw who was down on his luck, especially if he was locally known, getting a grubstake was not a problem. Many an outlaw (Butch

Cassidy, Elza Lay, the Sundance Kid, Matt Warner) was famous for paying back debts generously. People were eager to give them what they needed. Most of the outlaws came from solid, hard-working stock. They didn't put on airs, so the locals identified with them. They were sometimes viewed as Robin Hoods with six-guns—robbing those who preyed upon the poor.

Both ranchers and outlaws disliked the big cattle spreads, which were viewed as the common enemy. Such outfits were famous for being range hogs and swallowing up little outfits. Honest Brown's Hole ranchers believed rustling done against cattle barons was just cause and effect. Both the "midnight trail" riders and honest ranchers had a serious distrust for lawmen, banks, and the railroad.

As the saying goes, the Brown's Hole population "forked their own broncs"—handled their own problems. No lawmen were necessary or wanted.

Matt Warner (left) at age 21 with his outlaw friend Jim Peterson

Even in the late 1800s, Brown's Hole was one of the last wild, undeveloped pieces of real estate in the lower forty-eight states. Today, it's still a rugged place that seems to exist in another time. There are good populations of deer and elk. In the aspen forests there are bears and moose and mountain lions. There are rattlesnakes, prehistoric ruins, fossils, rocky plateaus, and deep picturesque canyons. The area is alive with history. This is a piece of the West that hasn't joined the age of the microchip.

Specifically, the valley is an ancient riverbed, roughly 6 miles long and running about 35 miles in a west-to-east direction. The term Brown's Hole is sometimes used to refer to any place in the region, not just the basin proper. Brown's Hole is in the northeastern corner of Utah, extending into western Colorado and southern Wyoming. Along the south are Diamond Mountain and the Green River. The rich grasslands on the edge of Cold Spring Mountain are ideal rangeland.

The Ute and Shoshone Indian tribes have frequented the valley for hundreds of years. Father Ortiz, arriving in 1650, was probably the first white man to visit the region. It wasn't rediscovered again until 1825, when William Ashley explored the lower sections. Two years later Kit Carson trapped and traded in the valley. By the 1830s it was known to a number of mountain men. A trapper named Baptise Brown worked the beaver-rich valley and got snowed in. It proved to be an excellent wintering spot since it was full of game, making winter hunting easy. The long valley was considerably warmer than the higher mountains—which got most of the snow.

It was called Brown's Hole after Baptise Brown and before long became a popular wintering spot. (*Hole* is a mountain man term for a valley or basin.) In the late 1830s two men named Thompson and Craig established a trading post they called Fort Davy Crockett. It did business for a few years until the beaver trade died out. In its day, the Crockett post was visited by the likes of Jim Bridger and most of the other famous mountain men.

John Wesley Powell floated the Green in 1869 and called the region Brown's Park instead of Brown's Hole. Informally, it goes by both names. Officially it's Brown's Park. To those who love the region, and to most of the early inhabitants, it's Brown's Hole.

After the decline of the beaver trade, the Hole remained a wintering area for trappers because of the abundance of other game. In the 1850s a few bandits who preyed on the overland trails would drive their stolen stock into the lower regions to winter. Later on, several gangs, including the Wild Bunch, called the region home at one time or another. Among these were the Rock Springs Gang, the Tom Crowley Gang, "Mexican Joe" Herrera's Gang, and the Bassett Gang.

The first ranchers arrived in the 1870s, when the large cattle herds were pushed up from Texas. Stockmen who wintered in the area discovered it was ideal cattle country. Surprisingly, the area was overlooked by the big ranching concerns that were ruthlessly gobbling up rangeland and pushing out small ranchers at gunpoint (even if they had been there first and had legal rights to the land). It was also supposed to be deeded Ute land. Because of the cattle barons' past practices in the region, settlers in the Hole had a natural dislike for these big outfits and felt that taking a few cows from a range hog to start one's herd was a morally justified act.

Wild cattle without brands, of course, were fair game and abundant. In addition, few large operations could keep all their cattle branded, and these mavericks, too, were fair game. If a few branded head were taken in the process, oh well. The rancher needing a stake would collect the strays, often on common rangeland, pushing the stock to his spread.

People such as Isom Dart, Matt Rash, Elizabeth Bassett, and Ann Bassett were blatant rustlers from time to time, pushing any animal they found into the Hole, then using a hot wire or a saddle ring to doctor up and change the brand.

Matt Rash was a top hand but a bit temperamental. Apocryphally, when he got fired from the K-Brand Ranch, he took a herd of 650 cattle

Group of Brown's Hole men, including Isom Dart (center)
Denver Public Library, Western History Collection

to Cold Spring Mountain, where his wagon wheel brand was artfully administered. His honor had been impugned, and he felt they owed him.

Brown's Hole was filled with a number of colorful people. The Bassett family lived in the area for more than one hundred years. In 1878 Herb and Elizabeth Bassett wintered with their Uncle Sam Bassett until the young couple could build a cabin of their own. During the winter Elizabeth gave birth to a daughter, Ann. Elizabeth had no milk, so she hired a Ute wet nurse to feed her little girl until spring, when the family finally procured a milking cow. As their ranching concerns prospered, the couple established a warm, friendly home that was open to travelers and friends alike. The down-and-out were always welcome, fed, and grubstaked.

Herb wasn't much of a rancher. He left that to his wife. He was a quiet, intellectual man who loved to read and play music. He had a large library in his home. Later, when he became the postmaster, he moved his books to a separate building. This was the first public library in the region. Visitors were welcome to pull up a chair and read as long as they liked. It is reported that Butch Cassidy was an avid reader and spent many hours with his nose in a book in Herb's library.

Elizabeth was an educated, genteel woman who could hold her own at a formal tea party if she wanted to. She was also a feminist in her own right and lobbied for women's rights—especially the vote. She was opinionated, stubborn, and loyal to her friends, but Elizabeth commanded an intense, filial loyalty in return. Men would do anything for her—especially the outlaw crowd she had so fully befriended. She was a cattle rancher and proud of it. Isom Dart was a very close friend. He and Matt Rash were principals in the Bassett Gang. While Elizabeth had a genteel manner, she could also be a tough frontier woman. She could out-bronco, out-lasso, out-rustle, and outshoot most men and she could also cuss a blue streak during a fit of temper.

When the local doctor died, supposedly the first natural death in the area, she took over his duties. She read his medical books and learned the trade. Elizabeth spent many nights ministering to the sick.

If someone crossed her, he was an enemy for life. The Hoy outfit is a good example. They were a high and mighty family, headed by a grouchy patriarch who acquired the family land questionably. Elizabeth wasn't above strapping on six-guns and heading off in the night to herd a few Hoy cattle onto her range or burn a few Hoy barns and line cabins. Elizabeth also hated the big ranches in Colorado. She had a special hatred for the Two Bar. The Bassett Gang followed her without question, causing mischief in that area.

She had fed, grubstaked, and befriended most of her gang at one time or another. They felt it a privilege to ride for her. It was reported that they were so loyal that they bragged about being willing to lay down their lives for Elizabeth if she asked.

One of her favorite hands was a cowboy named Jack Rollas. He was shot by a drifting Texas puncher and his two friends after the Bassett family had fed them. With a few gang hands, Elizabeth is said to have followed the killers and caught them. She brought them back to her ranch hog-tied. Rollas was dying from his wounds by this time, but Elizabeth handed the dying man her pistol and told him to shoot the three Texans for what they'd done. By this time, Jack was all done in and didn't have the strength to hold up the big Colt. Elizabeth threatened to shoot the murderers herself but Herb talked her into calling on the local law many miles away in Routt County. She thought this unnecessary but relented to keep her husband happy.

Knowing what might happen, Herb, who was the acting justice of the peace, went to the barn where the prisoners were bound. He told the men to saddle up, ride to Hahns Peak, Colorado, and turn themselves over to the sheriff. It didn't take the Texans more than a minute to make tracks. This was a lucky break, and a man didn't get too many around Elizabeth. They thought this crazy lady was going to shoot them. They naturally headed north to Rock Springs, Wyoming, with no intention of turning themselves in. Apparently they had been chasing Jack Rollas for two years, since Rollas had killed one of the Texans' brothers in a gunfight.

What Herb didn't know, or want to know, was that his Bible-reading wife and her Bassett Gang followed the unarmed Texans—or so the story goes. (It's hard to separate fact from fiction when it comes to Elizabeth since she truly has become larger than life.) Herb had kept their guns. The Bassett Gang caught up to the unarmed men in Irish Canyon, where they outnumbered the Texans three to one. Elizabeth officiated over the necktie party and the shallow, unmarked burial in a common grave. Legend has it she put the nooses over the condemned men herself.

Like their feisty mother, Elizabeth's girls were very beautiful, with more than a fair streak of the wild. Even expensive finishing schools couldn't take the range out of Herb's daughters. Like their mother, they were well educated, genteel, and properly mannered—if they wanted to be. Nevertheless, they loved to raise hell and get their own way. They were born to ride and shoot and borrow cattle if the notion took them— and no mere mortal man had better get in their way or try to saddle them. Both had long lines of suitors and knew how to use men.

Up on Red Creek lived a crusty old miner named Jess Ewing. He'd had a stroke of bad luck a few years back, when he had tangled with a young grizzly. Jess finally got the best end of the deal, but not before the bear raked his face with its front claws. He was a mean cuss besides being ugly to look at. Few people liked him—even fewer cared when he left this world. The scar didn't help his looks or his disposition. Being so grouchy, he couldn't get a proper woman in the normal way. He found a suitable wife at a mail-order outfit, paid his money, and took her to his best cabin near the Green River.

Before long, his wife, Madame Forrestall Ewing (she went by the name Madame), attracted the attention of a dashing young outlaw named Tom Duncan. He was "resting over" in the Hole, letting things cool down if the story is correct. Tom had been involved in a shooting at Rock Springs, and prudence dictated he lie low, avoiding those out to lynch him. While Madame was surely no beauty queen or spring chicken, there weren't a lot of women available in these parts.

Madame apparently wasn't fussy, but even she didn't think much of the miner husband she'd coupled up with. At one time she was said to have been a dance hall girl. Legend has it she also peddled rotgut whiskey, among other things.

One day she winked at Tom and he winked back. He conveniently rented a nearby cabin from the clawed-up miner. When Jess took off up Red Canyon to work his mine, the two would play patty-cake at the out- law's cabin. Miner Ewing got wise to his cheating wife and the young outlaw with a price on his head, so he snuck up to the canyon to bust in on the two preoccupied in the guilty pleasures of the flesh.

All Jess was packing was his bowie knife, perfect for carving up the two star-crossed lovers. But Mrs. Duncan hadn't raised a fool. By now, Tom had calculated that the old man knew of their tryst, so he was keeping an eye out—not wanting to be caught, literally, with his pants down. The last man Old Ewing had tangled with hadn't lived to see spring. Jess had sliced up his quasi-mining partner, a man named Robinson, after the two quarreled one winter over a claim. Legend has it that the mean old miner literally gutted poor Robinson with his trusty blade on the frozen ice of the Green River. He was about to use the same knife to teach Tom his last lesson.

While the old miner was slipping down the draw, Tom lined up on his chest with a big-bore buffalo gun. His shot was a little high, but it did the trick. Being a thoughtful outlaw, Tom took the miner's horses, his gold, and his woman. The lovers slipped out of the Hole after going down to the trading store to tell the folks the old man was ill and would need attending.

Madame and Tom no doubt deserved each other and were never heard from again. Jess wasn't too popular, and he wasn't mourned. John Jarvie, the storekeeper, buried Jess next to the gutted Robinson. Their graves can still be seen next to the Green River by the Jarvie store. Jess's mining claim has never been found. Brown's Hole still holds some secrets.

Isom Dart
The Black Rustler from Brown's Hole

Isom Dart, sometimes known as Black Isom, was one of the original settlers in Brown's Hole—probably arriving in the mid- to late 1870s.

A respected man and a top cowhand in anyone's book, he had a way with horses. His gentle-trained, hand-raised cow ponies were among the best in the Rocky Mountains. Isom was a patient man, a man beloved by local ranch children. It was not unusual for him to get down on his hands and knees and play with the kids for hours while the adults talked. He was a friendly sort, helpful at branding time or during roundups, a good fighter, an expert with a lariat.

Isom Dart was a skilled rustler (which also made him a respected man in the Hole). He could slip in and "take cattle out from under your nose." But that wasn't all. He was a noted artisan at doctoring brands with a hot iron or a saddle ring. He had a nice herd built up, thanks in part to Hoy and Two Bar cattle. Branding questionable stock was his specialty. At one time he was indicted in the Sweetwater country, but his case wasn't brought to trial.

Born in 1855, Isom was a former slave and a cowman from Texas. With his saddle partner, Matt Rash, Isom had helped push a herd to the northern prairies. When the cattle were sold, the two drifted south and found a niche in Brown's Hole. In that part of the West, Isom discovered, a man was judged more on his ability and less by the color of his skin.

Isom was a flashy dresser, wearing a floppy sombrero with a wide rattlesnake band. He sported a silk bandanna about his neck, and a large topaz ring graced his finger. He played a mouth organ and the fiddle and was often featured at the local dances, along with Matt Rash, who played the Mexican guitar.

As a loyal friend of the Bassett family, especially Elizabeth Bassett (matriarch of the Bassett clan), he was a member of the Bassett Gang—following Elizabeth on highly successful raids against the Two Bar and Hoy Ranches (neighbors she was feuding with). He was Elizabeth's right-hand man.

His daring rustling exploits, especially against the Two Bar in Colorado, were the toast of the local ranchers. After a while, Isom's midnight "cattle roundups" brought him to the attention of the baron ranchers whose herds he (along with Matt Rash) had lightened considerably. He'd rustled a few cattle too many. The big ranches put pressure on the Rock Springs sheriff to do something about "that damned nest of outlaws living in the Hole"—the worst being Black Isom. The sheriff was a sensible man who knew there was no way he'd ride into and out of Brown's Hole alive—let alone find Isom Dart. No lawman had ever ridden into those parts and ridden out alive. The good sheriff liked to drink whiskey, listen to the piano at the dance hall, and hunt antelope—things he couldn't do if he was pushing up sagebrush. It was a fool's errand, anyway.

To keep the big ranchers off his back, he talked an outlaw named Joe (in some accounts his name is listed as Jim) Philbrick into bringing the rustler Isom to trial. Never mind that Joe was wanted in three states and suspected of rustling in Wyoming. The sheriff kept the new appointment quiet so the news wouldn't spread, pinned the deputy badge on Joe Philbrick, gave him some traveling money, and wished him luck as he headed for the biggest nest of rustlers in the United States. He doubted that this temporary deputy would return alive. Chalk another one up to Brown's Hole, since Deputy Joe Philbrick, one-time outlaw, would never see Rock Springs again.

But sometimes it takes an outlaw to catch an outlaw.

Isom Dart

Denver Public Library, Western History Collection

No one is sure how Deputy Joe got the drop on the wily Isom Dart, but he did. It was likely Isom was on his own turf and had his guard down. No lawman had dared come into the Hole before. Joe had the drop, so the rustler went without a fuss. You don't argue with a cocked Colt six-gun. Joe tied Isom up and put him in his buckboard—which was a curious way to travel. Nearly everyone at that time rode on horseback because the roads were less than desirable for wheeled transport.

A day out of Rock Springs, on a steep section of rough road, the wagon slid off the track and tumbled down a gully. Isom managed to jump free as the buckboard flipped. The deputy wasn't so lucky. Joe was seriously hurt in the accident and pinned under the wagon. Isom loosened his tied hands and pried the wagon off the injured man with a pole. He dragged Joe free, stopped his bleeding, and tended to the man's injuries to the best of his abilities. When his patient was stable, he righted the wagon, gathered up the spooked stock, repaired the broken tack, and started off to Rock Springs as fast as he could. He knew that Joe had internal injuries and needed serious medical help. Nearly killing the poor horses, he got Joe to a doctor. He stopped, had a stiff drink, and turned himself in to the Rock Springs sheriff.

He was promptly thanked for his heroics and jailed.

When Deputy Joe started to mend, he vowed he would do all he could to get Isom out of jail. Isom could have freed himself, but he had put his life in jeopardy to help the man who was bringing him in to trial—and that meant something to a westerner. Joe said that he'd shoot the sheriff or break Isom out of jail himself if he had to. Most of the townsfolk felt the same way. Isom had showed moral character, and that certainly overshadowed any crimes he may or may not have committed.

Isom Dart came to trial in Rock Springs a couple of weeks later.

Deputy Joe testified in his favor. It didn't take the jury long to find the man not guilty. Few of the townspeople, including the sheriff, cared much for the big cattle bosses anyway. At that time in the West, it was rare for a local jury, usually composed of workingmen—most of whom had taken a few cows when no one was looking—to convict a fellow of "borrowing cattle" from a man who could afford to miss them (and who probably stole them "legally," himself).

Isom had some drinks with the locals and headed back a free man to his ranch and his growing herd in Brown's Hole. The large ranchers in southwestern Wyoming and northwestern Colorado were quickly losing faith in the criminal justice system. They could bring a cattle thief to trial, but it was difficult to get him convicted by an unsympathetic jury.

Two could play this deadly game of frontier chess. If the courts wouldn't help the large ranches clean up the range, they'd be forced to take the law into their own hands. Yes, the large cattle barons were often ruthless and immoral in their practices. Yes, they frequently rode rough-shod over smaller ranching concerns who couldn't stand up to their political clout or their hired gunslinging cowboys. Yes, they yielded little local sympathy and too often administered their own brand of justice. Men like Tom Horn, so-called range detectives, charged up to six hundred dollars a body. There were no juries to contend with, and a bullet had a finality of its own. Of Tom Horn it was said, "He had a method that never failed." If the law wouldn't do its job, the big cattlemen could find someone who would.

Isom Dart didn't know it, but when he saw two men riding off Cold Spring Mountain near the draw where he was hiding, it was the beginning of the end. He knew the two men: Matt Rash and his new summer hand, a man named Hicks. They were coming off the summer range. Isom noted that Hicks was tall and weathered, and he rode a horse like a man born in the saddle. Isom liked him.

Hicks was good with stock. It appeared that Matt had hired himself a good hand. When Isom and Matt had played at the schoolhouse dance the previous Saturday, Hicks had joined in with his mouth organ. Later, he stood his two new friends at least four stiff drinks. You had to like a man who wasn't tight with his whiskey. The next day, Isom showed Hicks where Matt's line cabin was in the high country.

As Isom was leaving the mountain, Hicks offered to buy the sorrel gelding he was riding. The pony might have been the best cow horse in the basin. Matt, too, had tried to buy the horse a number of times—even though he knew it wasn't for sale. Isom had raised the pony from a bottle, and he'd have sooner lost an arm than part with it. Hicks didn't miss much with those deep eyes of his—he knew a good horse.

As the two men rode up the trail, Isom pointed his Winchester and half-heartedly said, "I'll shoot ya if ya comin' up fath'r."

Matt knew Isom wouldn't shoot, so he nosed his horse up the draw and saw what Isom was trying to hide. A dead animal was lying in the gully. It was a roan shorthorn, Sam Spicer's prize breeding bull. Old Man Spicer, a crusty sort, had spread a bunch of rumors about Isom. There'd been bad blood between them for a long time. No doubt, shooting the animal was Isom's way of getting back.

Isom cocked his Winchester in a threatening manner—something he shouldn't have done when facing his friend. Like lightning, Matt drew his six-shooter and shot a hole in the stock of the weapon, not appreciating Isom's gesture. Hicks and Isom were a little stunned at how fast he'd pulled his pistol and fired.

"You got one chance," Matt grinned, looking at his smoking Colt. "Go tell Sam about your shooting his bull and pay him 'fore he hunts you down with that buffalo gun. If ya want me to keep mum and take yore chances—I won't tell. But I'll be wanting that sorrel horse of yours as payment for my silence."

Isom wasn't going to tell Sam Spicer about the bull and Matt knew it. Nor was he going to give Matt his best horse to keep quiet. Later, Matt would take the prized cow pony when Isom wasn't looking. He'd tell the Hole folks he'd bought it. Isom couldn't press the issue since Matt would tell about him shooting the bull. Isom wasn't happy about how things turned out, but he'd wait and let the bull issue die down, then he'd steal back his horse when Matt had his back turned.

During these few weeks, Hicks had seen and heard enough to convict both Isom and Matt. Hick's real name was Tom Horn, and he was undercover to get the goods on the worst rustlers in the Hole. Specifically, he had been sent to collect evidence on Matt Rash and Isom Dart. He'd first worked for Sam Spicer, owner of the bull. He despised Spicer and didn't care about the shorthorn—the old man deserved it for badmouthing. But he now had hard evidence on Isom and Matt for rustling.

The jury was in. Both men were guilty, and Tom knew what to do—Matt first, then Isom.

It happened during a chilly autumn. It had been four months since Isom had plugged Spicer's bull in the draw at the bottom of Cold Spring Mountain. Tom had since executed Matt Rash. Now the leaves were turning, and there was a heavy frost each morning. The elk bulged. Winter wasn't far off. At first Isom had been blamed for Matt's murder, the way Tom had planned it. Isom's name had been circulated in the Brown's Hole rumor mill, but after the initial investigation, few considered him a suspect in Matt's death.

The locals had come to realize that Hicks was really the killer Tom Horn. After shooting Matt, Tom had walked out to the corral and put a bullet in the horse he'd tried to buy earlier. Folks knew Isom had raised and trained that pony and loved it. Isom surely wasn't the killer since he'd never shoot a fine pony.

On October 4, partway up Cold Spring Mountain, Isom's good friends, including the Bassett brothers and Billy Rash, were visiting. Everyone was still a little jumpy since Matt's murder. They hadn't seen Tom for months, so they hoped he'd left the country. It was chilly that morning as Isom walked out to the woodpile to get fuel for their breakfast fire. The Bassett brothers were coming out the door for some extra armloads. They were laughing and telling stories. In the still, frosty air, two shots rang out so fast that at first they sounded like one. The first slug took Isom in the face, killing him instantly. As he was falling, a second bullet ripped a hole in his chest. The Bassett brothers were frightened and ran for the safety of the cabin, where they spent the rest of the day. They slipped out the next evening by sawing a hole in the back of the shack.

Later, two .30-30 cases were found next to a ponderosa pine a little over a hundred yards from the cabin. It was obvious who'd killed Isom. The .30-30 Winchester was Tom's calling card.

Tenderly, the murdered man was wrapped in a blanket and buried near his cabin. The funeral words were spoken by the fiery Ann Bassett. She prayed for God to strike Tom Horn dead for this poor man's murder and for the murder of her betrothed, Matt Rash.

After Isom Dart was laid to rest, the Two Bar and other ranches noticed a significant decrease in their cattle losses.

Tom Horn
The System That Never Fails

Tom Horn said, "Dead men don't steal no cattle." He took a last drag and rubbed the cowboy cigarette on a smooth rock. Tom had watched Matt Rash's line cabin for the last two hours. Above all, he was a patient man. In another life, he'd lived contentedly with the Apache—even taking a native wife. During the Apache Wars, he'd served as a scout for the U. S. Army. He'd been a guide, a tracker, and a man hunter. From his adopted Indian father, he'd learned patience. He'd also learned how to track and live off the land without being seen.

He could follow a man across slickrock if he had to and could disappear, leaving no sign, apparently dropping off the face of the landscape. Tom knew a trail could not be rushed—it didn't matter if you were chasing bronco Apaches in Sonora or trailing a cattle thief. He'd told this to the great Indian fighter General Crook, a man he respected. He'd tried to tell it to General "Bear Coat" Miles, who took over Crook's job. Miles hadn't listened.

Tom mused as he tightened the cinch on his worn saddle. His favorite horse, Pacer, was full on mountain grass and the oats he had brought. He was ready to ride—and ride he must as soon as this job was over. He checked the legs on the big horse, then the shoes. He'd be covering 50 miles across rough country so he could have an alibi for his whereabouts. The West was changing and so was his way of life. You couldn't just kill a man, even if he deserved it, and let it go at that.

Tom Horn
Denver Public Library, Western History Collection

Maybe he'd go back to Arizona and look for his wife and son when this job was over. It'd been years since he'd seen them. He'd been truly happy only when he'd lived with Nopal and her people. He wanted to see their son, Sombre. Tom thought of Geronimo, Chato, Nana, Mickey Free, Old Pedro, and the others. He had taken his young Nopal from Geronimo, which had caused bad feelings between the two. Later, he'd been there when Geronimo surrendered. The Apache had a good way of life and were fighting for it. Bear Coat had lied to them all—the warriors as well as the blue-coated soldiers sent to bring them in. Apaches good and bad had been loaded indiscriminately into the steam cars and sent off to Florida to die like rats.

In the years since the wars, he'd been a Pinkerton, a stockman, and a Rough Rider for Teddy Roosevelt. But mostly he'd been a "range detective" for the big cattle outfits. He was always hunting men, it seemed, one way or another.

It was nearly time to approach the cabin. There were no windows in the line shack. He'd come down from the back. He liked Cold Spring Mountain—it reminded him of the high country in the Southwest the Apache loved. The feel of summer was in the air, and life was blooming all about him. He would exact a proper and just punishment on the guilty Matt Rash, a criminal, and slip away. Maybe he'd get drunk for a week to get the bad taste out of his mouth.

The way he'd planned it, the blame should fall on Matt's friend, Isom Dart.

The sun was now straight up in the corn-blue sky. Tom was beginning to feel his age. The clump of aspen that hid him was 300 yards up the slope. When he saw smoke coming out of the weathered, black pipe made from old tin cans, he knew Matt was making his noonday lunch.

Tom ran his hand over his face, a face brown and wrinkled by the wind and sun. His hair was starting to turn gray. Slipping off his boots, he secured them to the horn of his saddle. Tom rode barefooted until he was 75 yards from the shack. Like the Apache he knew and respected, he made his way noiselessly toward the condemned—ignoring the sharp rocks against his feet. Pacer was ground-hitched and waiting.

It was sad in a way. Tom liked Matt, outlaw though he was. Matt was a good cowboy and a skilled hand with stock. He was playful and pleasant—quick with a funny story. But he was first and last a cattle thief. Ora Ben Haley, owner of the Two Bar Ranch, had hired Tom to do a job, and he would do it. He rode for the brand. It was no secret that many of Matt's cows had come from the Two Bar. Matt openly bragged about it.

What was it that Matt liked to sing after a few tin cups of whiskey? "We thank God for our bread and Ora Ben Haley for our meat." Matt bragged that anyone who sat down for a meal at his table had meat with his beans—but it wouldn't be Matt Rash's beef.

When Tom had come into the Hole, he'd worked for Old Man Sam Spicer for two months. Spicer was a stingy old man, and Tom disliked him. But working for Spicer got Tom, who was going by the name of Hicks, in with the Brown's Hole regulars. He'd met Matt Rash and Dart Isom at a dance and gotten on well with them. Matt had hired Hicks to look after seven hundred head of stock on his Cold Spring Mountain summer range. Besides, Matt wanted to work on his new cabin since he and Ann Bassett ("Queen of the Rustlers") were to be married soon.

Hicks had ridden with Matt. They'd shared many a campfire tale, played music at the local schoolhouse dance, talked about women, and drank.

But that didn't matter now. Matt Rash was going to die for his sins.

He was a cattle rustler, and Tom had been hired to clean up Brown's Hole. He'd ridden long enough with Matt to see him rustle cattle from Wyoming and Colorado ranches. He'd seen him put his hot wagon wheel brand over other brands. He had plenty of proof. Tom had standards. He would never kill a man in cold blood. He was a hard man, but he was governed by a private code of ethics: "Don't kill 'em unless you're sure they're guilty. You personally have to catch 'em at it."

Tom had nothing but respect for any sort of hardworking people. Once during a "norther" just outside of Denver, he saw a group of dirt-poor immigrant settlers getting off the train. The families were so destitute that the children had to go barefoot in the January snow. Tom gathered up the kids, took them into the general store, and bought them shoes, socks, and winter coats. He hustled them to a restaurant and fed them. After the kids were full, he marched them back to their folks and rode off into the blizzard after some rustlers. The men he chased were never seen again.

His heart went out to poor settlers and ranchers. He respected them and would help a man with his last dollar. Tom, however, had no tolerance for thieves—especially cattle thieves. One time near Laramie, he spent several months building an airtight case against the Langhoff rustlers. After careful planning, he caught the cattle thieves in the act. Tom took care to disarm the rustlers and brought them to justice. The facts of the case were obvious, and the sentencing should have been sure.

Nevertheless, only one rustler got any sort of sentence. The others got a few days in jail and a token fine. These were the last men he brought in . . . alive.

If the criminal justice system was flawed, there were other ways of meting out justice. He had a system that never failed. He never moved until he was completely sure the person in question was a criminal. He had to satisfy himself of their guilt—no matter what his employer had said. He collected the evidence personally, and if it was damning, so be it. Then, before he moved, he gave the thief a chance to leave. Usually this was in the form of a letter. He would tell the guilty party he would be killed if he didn't leave the country in one week.

To this range detective, his work wasn't murder. It was justice.

Matt Rash was convicted—even if he, Range Detective Tom Horn, was jury, judge, and executioner. Tom loosened his belly gun from the holster. He cocked the Colt before he got to the house so there would be no noise. Tom had seen Matt draw, and the man was very fast and accurate. Tom was fast with a handgun, as he'd proved many times, but he knew Matt was better. He wasn't going to take a chance.

Tom slipped around the cabin and into the open door. He previously had warned Matt and hoped he'd leave. It would make his job a lot simpler.

Matt never knew what happened. He was not alarmed since the man who stood in the lighted doorway was his friend—even if there was a cocked Colt in his hand. He was probably going to invite his friend to lunch when the pistol barked—the report was quite loud in such a small cabin. In disbelief, he saw the arc of flame and felt the strange sensation burning in his chest as he fell to the ground in a state of shock.

Tom noted that his first shot was a little high.

At this point, the reports of what happen differ. Some have Tom shooting Matt in the chest a second time as the mortally wounded man tried to pull himself up to the table. Other accounts have Tom shooting Matt in the face point blank.

Because of the nature of the wounds, most historians feel that Tom moved the dead or dying Matt to his bunk, took off his boots, covered him with a blanket, and hung his gun belt on a nail. Then he took Matt's money, twenty-four dollars in bills, rolled the notes, and stuck them near his head. Some accounts have the critically wounded Matt dragging himself to his bed, hanging his gun up, and removing his boots—but this doesn't seem likely given the man's condition.

As Tom left, he put a bullet in the prize cow pony Matt had taken from his friend Dart Isom. Tom thought this act would place suspicion for the murder on Dart; however, as he'd learn later, the plan backfired. The horse was one of the best ponies he'd ever seen. It probably troubled him more to put a bullet in the cutting horse than it did to shoot the rustler.

It didn't matter if the courts would not convict cattle rustlers because Tom Horn and his famous .30-30 Winchester or his Colt .45 would.

Near the end of the century, the Stock Growers Association had become powerful politically and legally—if not financially. Nevertheless, Brown's Hole was still untamed. It had become a rustler's no-man's-land that was almost impossible to penetrate. Hole rustlers plundered ranches in three states. As at Robber's Roost, outlaws and stolen stock came and went without censure. For the most part, the outlaw contingent left the honest ranchers in Brown's Hole and the surrounding areas alone. Range-baron cattle, however, were fair game.

Those on the dodge—stock thieves, robbers—quickly learned that they couldn't survive without the goodwill of the locals. Many a God-fearing rancher who wouldn't steal a thimble would willingly provide horses and supplies for an outlaw on the dodge. Outlaws, in turn, sold stock with "questionable" ownership well below market value to such ranchers. Most outlaws were also good ranch hands, and while they "laid over" in the no-man's-land, they often helped the locals with ranch chores, branding, and roundups. Butch Cassidy, Matt Warner, the Sundance Kid, Elza Lay, and others were known for pitching in—usually for the price of a good meal. Outlaws were good neighbors and thus insulated by the honest folk.

Large cattle outfits wanted the rustlers dealt with. They also wanted the land itself. Because of the rugged nature of the real estate and the independent nature of the ranchers, Brown's Hole was still one of the last untapped ranges in the West. The big outfitters looked enviously at the basin as a wonderful new piece of property to perpetuate their feudal expansion. If they could wipe out the outlaws, they could step in with their strong-arm tactics and hired guns and push out the small ranchers—as they'd done so often before—claiming the land for themselves. They wanted to brand this range for their own before it was too late.

There had always been trouble with the eastern borders of the Hole, but things heated to a head in the 1890s.

It was not surprising when the manager of the Two-Circle Bar, Wilson Carey, suggested to several other big ranchers that they all put up

Tom Horn in prison
Wyoming State Archives

two hundred dollars a month into a pool to "clean up the range"—starting with Brown's Hole. The other association members agreed and put their money on the line. They wouldn't have to do their own dirty work. The money was given to Charles Ayer, so he could hire a really effective range detective—the man whose system never failed. Enter Tom Horn.

They got what they paid for.

Tom was known to be fiercely loyal to his employers, a hard man who knew how to handle their hard problem. Tom was fearless. Once when drunk, he took a punch at the famous prizefighter Gentleman Jim Corbett after calling him out. He spent nineteen days in a Denver hospital afterward, with a broken jaw for his whiskey-clouded foolishness.

Before taking the most extreme measures, Tom was noted for warning the guilty party. Maybe this eased his conscience. Why shoot a man if he'd get up and leave? Many did. In Brown's Hole, besides warning Matt Rash and Isom Dart, Tom warned Mel Triplett with a note nailed to his cabin door: "You've ate your last Two Bar beef. You got one week to get out." To another rustler on Crouse Creek, he tacked a note in the outhouse that read, "Two Bar beef is poison—you have one week." For a couple of rustlers in Hoy Canyon he hung a bag of salt with two rocks in it to a kitchen lamp with a curt note: "Put these under you head." (Tradition has it that Tom put rocks under the heads of the men he shot as his calling cards.)

Between jobs, Tom was a braggart and a drunk who spent his money in honky-tonks and red-light districts. Whiskey talk and his desire to look important would finally catch up to him. When he was working, though, he was one of the finest trackers in the American West. As a stock detective, few were more effective or his equal.

There were two sides to the range conflict. Rustling was certainly a serious problem, if not at times a plague, to large ranchers. Many ranchers went bust as a result. Smaller stockmen and settlers, even townsfolk, had the habit of viewing large cattle herds as their personal walking food supply—if not a quick way to build up one's own herd. At the same time, the large outfits frequently ran their ranches like feudal estates, with might making right. Many a small ranch with good bottomland, prime winter range, or water was just a pawn to be absorbed into a larger power play. Large outfits even rustled some themselves. Many large spreads were built on stolen herds they had "absorbed." The large ranchers had money and armed riders, as well as legal clout, and bullied to get their way.

For some reason, Tom sided with the large outfits. He did what he thought was right. Stealing cows was a crime.

He once told a rancher friend, "Killing is my specialty—I look upon it as a business proposition." And he did. To him, taking care of rustlers was not a lot different than shooting wolves or lions threatening a herd. By the turn of the century, though, the West was redefining itself. His methods were no longer politically correct. Public pressure was turning against such violent strong-arm tactics.

In the end, Tom was hung for killing a fourteen-year-old boy, Willie Nickell, in eastern Wyoming. It is likely that young Willie was not murdered by Tom. Flat-out murder would go against his established patterns of operation.

Tom was likely railroaded, if not literally sacrificed, by the stockmen he had faithfully served. The evidence against him was twisted and manufactured. His confession—the confession that drove the nails into his coffin—should have been inadmissible. It appears that Marshal Joe LeFores (a famous trailer of Butch Cassidy and the Sundance Kid) got Tom drunk and manipulated the transcript to indicate his guilt. According to LeFores, Tom made a number of self-incriminating statements. Perhaps the worst was, "It was the best shot I ever made and the dirtiest trick I ever done." This remark was very likely taken completely out of context.

Nevertheless, Tom Horn swung, and with his execution ended a chapter of the Old West.

The Sundance Kid
The Gunfighter's Reputation

The Sundance Kid often called Utah home. He liked the land, and he liked the people. At least for a while, it was a haven from posses and lawmen. He came to escape, relax, and hide. Other than some rustling, he committed few crimes in the Beehive State's boundaries.

The Kid's real name was Harry Alonzo Longabaugh. He was born around April 1868. There was a fire in the courthouse in Mont Clare, Pennsylvania, so there are no official records. His birthday might be a year or two off either way. Young Harry was the last of five children brought up in a strict, God-fearing home. His father, a farmer, was a Civil War veteran who had served with the Union army. In the Longabaugh home, God was a northerner, and strict rules were needed to keep one on the straight and narrow.

Like all farm boys in his day, Harry could handle a rifle and a shotgun. Marksmanship came easy for him. He enjoyed hunting and shooting and being out in the woods. Young Longabaugh also liked school and was a better-than-average student. He loved to read and enjoyed the study of history. He even joined a literary group in 1882. He had a keen interest in Shakespeare, and his attitudes were somewhat more liberal than his folks appreciated. He read the classics, but he also had a passion for dime novels and could be considered a romantic. He was especially fond of stories that dealt with the West. More than anything else, the young lad dreamed of going to the territories and becoming a cowboy. He also wanted to be a gunfighter, an Indian fighter, and an explorer.

Harry Longabaugh (the Sundance Kid) and Etta Place in 1901
Pinkerton Archives

As a schoolboy, Harry seemed to get in his fair share of fights. Besides the black eyes and bruised knuckles, this activity always brought a scolding from his mother. Harry had a short fuse, so his mother encouraged him to work on his temper. Once he was pushed to a certain point, he flew off the handle and was unmanageable. While he had a small, close circle of friends, he didn't mind being alone, and some considered him a bit of a loner. Like his famous partner-to-be, he was a loyal man—to his friends and family, especially his older sister.

The siren call of the West, however, was too much. When he was fourteen years old, he left Pennsylvania for Colorado and adventures in the real West. In 1882 he hugged his beloved sister, Samana, wished his family a farewell, and went to live out his dream. He traveled by train and later by covered wagon to reach his cousin's ranch near Cortez, Colorado. The aspiring young westerner helped around the ranch for a while, but he had a wandering heart, and he didn't want to stay in one place when there was so much to see. He wanted to experience this exciting new world he'd inherited, so he moved around from ranch to ranch. This was not uncommon, as much of the available ranch work was seasonal.

He embraced the West and the cowboy trade. He learned his craft quickly and soon mastered it. He became a top hand in anyone's book. He took to ranch work and livestock as if he had been born to it. The future Sundance Kid drifted down to New Mexico. By now he could call himself a cowboy. He had a way with stock, especially horses, and was soon working as a horseman, a highly competitive position. He was indeed living out his dream and was eager to see the vast land called the American West before it was roped and tamed.

After a while, he rode north to Utah. He might have been tired of the range war he found himself in near Springer, New Mexico. He took work at the Lacy Cattle Company south of Monticello, Utah. The LC was one of Utah's very large spreads, with nearly fifteen thousand head on its ranges in various canyons. He worked as a horseman, breaking stock, and did some cowboy work during the slack time. Like all hands on the LC, he did his share of chasing rustlers. His ranch foreman at that time was a capable man named Bill Ball. Ball was shot to death by cattle thieves while young Harry was working for him. Not long after Ball's murder, Harry drifted up to the LaSal Mountains near Moab and worked for the Pittsburgh Land and Cattle Company, another large Utah ranch. Utah was developing into an important range at this time, although most of the ranches were considerably smaller than the two he had worked for. In the early part of the 1880s, there were 150,000 head of cattle in the Utah Territory. Within five years, the number of cattle had doubled to nearly 300,000 head. There was always a job for a good cowboy.

Ranch life was hard work, but when the day was done, the hands would hang about the bunkhouse, drink coffee, talk, or shoot their guns. There was a lot of target shooting going on, since many cowboys were vain about their marksmanship. By the time he was in his mid-teens, legend has it that the young lad could outshoot most any cowboy on the ranches he worked on. He was good with a rifle, but it was while he was a ranch hand in New Mexico and Utah that he learned and mastered the finer points of a Colt Peacemaker. He was also a quick study on the elements of the fast draw. Ironically, he couldn't afford his own handgun at this time.

A new Colt .45 cost one to two months' salary for a cowhand. For a lad who had grown up on the dime novels of his day, reading about Wild Bill and Buffalo Bill and the other gunslinging heroes of the pulp novel, this was living. No doubt he was saving up for his first pistol and gun belt with every paycheck. At any rate, he was very accurate on the fast draw (it's rather difficult to hit a target with any accuracy when one quick draws, so this skill was noteworthy). And he was reported to be very fast. Shooting this way came second nature to him.

He drifted back to the Cortez area again, to visit his cousin and family. At this time he might have become acquainted directly or indirectly with Butch Cassidy, Matt Warner, and Tom McCarty through horse racing. Harry was a good trainer and a skilled jockey himself. Horse circles in the intermountain West were not that large. Butch, Matt, and Tom were working a four- or five-county circuit with their racehorses, so it's likely that he at least knew who they were (and they him).

After a while, racing got old and times got tough. Harry took a job pushing a herd from Texas to Montana.

In the mid-1880s, the restless young hand headed north. He worked on a ranch near Culbertson, Montana. He left and drifted down to Wyoming. He was between riding jobs and was hungry. Things were getting desperate. He lived off what he had saved. Then he started to sell off his possessions one at a time for eating money, waiting for something to come up the following spring. On February 27, 1887, broke, hungry, and cold, he became desperate.

The drought of 1886 had been severe, so ranches weren't hiring. Following the drought came the Great Blizzard of 1886–87—one of the worst winters on record in Montana and Wyoming. In early November the first storm hit. The temperature was below zero, and soon 6 to 8 inches of snow covered the ground. This snow was followed by storm after storm. At one time in January, it snowed more than an inch per hour. During another blizzard that January, it snowed for three straight days and nights without letup. Some snowbanks in gullies were said to be 70 feet deep. Houses, cabins, and barns were sometimes completely covered. The herds weren't in good shape to begin with because of the tough summer. The range and the necessary feed were limited. Cattle were dying, their frozen bodies littering the range like the leftovers of a buffalo shoot.

The situation was desperate. There were few jobs. Harry became a thief—possibly to survive. Until this time we have no evidence to suggest that he was anything but an honest cowpoke and horseman.

He took a six-gun from James Widner. From Alonzo Craven he took a horse, a bridle, and a saddle. Both were cowhands at the VVV Ranch near Crook County, Wyoming. Sheriff Jim Ryand was on Harry's trail immediately. For the first time in his life—and certainly not the last—he was on the run. He dodged Sheriff Ryand for four months. He was captured once but escaped. He was finally caught near Miles City, Montana. While he was running from the law, similar robberies occurred that were subsequently blamed on him.

For a wanted man, the future Sundance Kid had a lot to learn about being careful. He was new at this sort of thing. He should have left northeastern Wyoming, but he didn't. Sheriff Ryand caught up with him for the first time on April 12 and took him aboard a train. Ryand wasn't a trusting man, but he had only three locks on his prisoner. The good sheriff felt the call of nature and left, thinking his captured thief couldn't get away, chained up as he was. Before the sheriff returned, Harry had picked the three locks and jumped from the train. This was the first of several miraculous escapes from the law. He said he felt like the train was going 100 miles per hour when he leaped to freedom.

This close call should have convinced Harry to leave Wyoming, but he continued to hang about the area. Finally Ryand caught up with him. It was personal for the sheriff this time. He'd looked quite silly when his prisoner got away while he was in the head with his pants down. The sheriff took the thief to Sundance, Wyoming, for his trial. His prisoner was locked up and guarded very carefully this time, Ryand fearing he would escape again.

Harry was upset by the way the newspapers were treating him before his trial. He had admitted to the crime he committed against the two cowhands at the VVV but denied the others he was accused of. In jail awaiting trial, hoping to set the record straight, he wrote the following letter to the editor of the *Daily Yellowstone Journal* on June 9, 1887:

> In your issue of June 7th, I read a very sensational and partly untrue article, which places me before the public not even second to the notorious Jesse James. Admitting that I have done

wrong and expecting to be dealt with according to law and not by false reports from parties who should blush with shame to make them, I ask a little space to set my case before the public in a true light. In the first place, I have always worked for an honest living; was employed last summer by one of the best outfits in Montana and don't think they can say aught against me, but having got discharged last winter, went to the Black Hills to seek employment—which I could not get . . . .

After this my course of outlawry commenced, and I suffered terribly for the want of food in the hope of getting back south without being detected. . . . Contrary to the statement in the *Journal*, I deny having stolen any horses. . . .

The young man went to trial with a public defender. At first he entered a not guilty plea, but he later changed it to guilty when the saddle, bridle, and pistol thefts were dropped in a plea bargain. He decided to skip the jury trial and have the judge pass sentence. He was charged and convicted of horse theft. On August 5, 1887, he was sentenced to two years of hard labor. Since the Laramie prison was full, he got lucky. The state of Wyoming contracted with the Sundance jail to keep the prisoner (it was paid $4.20 a week to keep him; an additional fee of $2.00 was paid for clothing). Other governmental sources kicked in more funding.

In February 1889, Territorial Governor Thomas Moonlight pardoned him, so he was fully vested in his civil rights. The governor's pardon read: "He's still under 21 years of age and his behavior has been good since confinement, showing an earnest desire to reform and . . . the sheriff, clerk, court . . . and others have this day made application to me to grant unto the said Harry Longabaugh a pardon of said crime of which he stands convicted."

He walked out of the jail a free man. For the next few years he drifted. He headed down to Cortez, Colorado, for a visit with his cousin. From this point on, his sobriquet was the Sundance Kid—in satirical honor of the town where he'd been tried and done time. Some have suggested that Sundance might have been the extra man in the 1889 Telluride, Colorado, bank robbery. Telluride is only 80 miles from Cortez, where he stayed with kin. They conclude that as a horseman and horse racer in that area, Sundance obviously knew Tom McCarty, Matt Warner, and Butch Cassidy, who might have invited him to be in on the heist. They suggest that Sundance was identified by name as the bandits fled (even if he wasn't on the official Wanted poster). Additionally, in Longabaugh family lore, the escaping outlaws took shelter at George Longabaugh's ranch in Cortez. George Longabaugh's wife, Mary, supposedly fed the outlaws a number of times.

It is possible that Sundance helped rob the Telluride bank. He had just spent nearly two years in jail, and his worldview had changed. However, the evidence of his involvement is only circumstantial. Maybe more information will come to light at a later date. As suggested, he likely knew the soon-to-be-famous members of the McCarty Gang, but at this time in his life, this kind of criminal participation seems out of character. He was a minor rustler in those days, not a bank robber. Matt Warner, in his biography, doesn't mention Sundance being involved.

After leaving Cortez, Sundance rode the grub line in the Powder River country, working here and there. He also rode with a few different rustling outfits, stealing cattle and horses as the occasion arose. He drifted through Colorado, Utah, Wyoming, and Montana. He had a few scrapes but nothing too serious. Nevertheless, the crowd he started to hang with was a little bit rougher and more questionable than those he'd previously been seen with.

He started to hone his shooting skills. He was already an excellent shot, but he worked on his draw speed. He'd been out of practice for two years. Those who knew him at the time said he stayed away from trouble, but he already had a reputation as someone to avoid. He was a bad man to tangle with in a fight—especially a gunfight.

Throughout his career, he was known as a serious gunfighter, but he surely didn't have a killer's instinct. While he was in jail awaiting trial, a newspaper reporter said he was a young Jesse James. Sundance was not flattered by the comparison. In fact, he was offended. He had developed a quiet confidence about his skill with Samuel Colt's equalizer. But he wasn't eager to have a reputation as a killer.

Ironically, while considered a gunfighter, he very likely never killed anyone in the Old West—at least there is no record that he did. Apparently, he was so good that no one wanted to cross him, or he finally learned how to control his temper.

He spent time in Alberta, Canada, working at the Bar U Ranch near Calgary. He is recorded on the Canadian Dominion census. Further accounts confirm that he attended the wedding (and was best man) of a good friend who was the ranch foreman. During the winter of 1892, he went into business at the Grand Central Hotel Saloon in Calgary. The partnership soon dissolved and he moved on.

Until November 29, 1892, Sundance's crimes never went beyond livestock rustling. However, he was about to change his professional status. Harry A. Longabaugh, drifter, cowhand, horseman, would become the Sundance Kid, a wanted criminal. There would be no going back.

With Bill Madden, an out-of-work puncher he had known back in 1884 near Cortez, and another jobless cowhand named Harry Bass, he held up the Great Northern train just outside Malta, Montana. The desperados climbed onto the first car, often referred to as the blind baggage car. They pulled the robbery in the wee hours of the night when it was dark (the train was on its way from St. Paul to Butte). The robbery had a number of comic elements about it. This was their first job, and they weren't very good at this crime business. It was an amateur effort. It wasn't well planned or thought through.

While they were holding up the train and shoving their Colts on the rail agent, their bandannas kept falling down. The agent got a good look at all three of the outlaws. (He was able to give such detailed descriptions that Bass and Madden were quickly captured.) Two outlaws took the agent to the express car while the third kept watch. There were several safes. They had the fellow open up two small safes—they got a whopping nineteen dollars plus change from one and six dollars from the other. When they told the agent to open the large safe, he said he couldn't. He said only a few officials along the route had the combination. Whether or not this was true, and it probably was, they seemed quite discouraged and went back to collect their partner with a staggering twenty-five bucks (some accounts say it was closer to seventy).

More experienced bandits might have threatened the agent with bodily harm to see if he was bluffing. Or more likely they would have planned for this contingency and had a few sticks of TNT handy. To make the job pay, most bandits would have at least robbed the agent and possibly some of the passengers, too.

This robbery was pulled off with little forethought. The disappointed trio rode away into the dark with pocket change. Madden and Bass enjoyed a few days of freedom. On December 1 at ten in the evening, because of the clear description given by the railway agent, the two were taken into custody while drinking in the local saloon. Sundance had the good sense at least to get out of town. Madden, thinking it would help him, confessed to their crimes almost at once and fingered all of his partners. Because of the description and since the law knew his name, Sundance was now a wanted man. He learned about the five-hundred-dollar reward on his head and he took off, eventually heading south. There's a good chance that he might have been scared straight after this fiasco if he hadn't been fingered by his partner.

Shortly after their arrest, Madden and Bass were taken to Great Falls, Montana, for trial and were sentenced to ten years in prison. Both were released a few years later for good behavior. One dropped out of western history, and the other was killed in a gunfight in 1895.

Since Sundance was now a wanted criminal, he figured he ought to start acting like one. He headed for the safety of Brown's Hole. He'd been there before, but now as a wanted man he appreciated the "don't ask, don't tell" philosophy of the basin. He was well liked and made a number of close friends among the ranchers and settlers, as well as the outlaw contingent. Before long, he became a trusted member of a semi-organized group of outlaws. He liked Utah and the region and was glad to be back among friends. Sundance did a share of rustling at this time to keep the financial wolves away. He hung with all the regulars, including Kid Curry and Butch Cassidy. In 1897, after the famous meeting at Cassidy Point, he took off with Kid Curry to hold up the Butte County Bank in Belle Fourche, South Dakota. This bank was less than 30 miles from Sundance, Wyoming. This area was his old stomping grounds, and he knew the territory well.

Like his first robbery, the Belle Fourche job turned into a disaster—this time the disaster was far more serious and potentially more deadly. It was better planned than the train robbery—but not much better. He and his crew were still pretty inexperienced at this sort of thing. Some of the men were at best flaky. The outlaws planned to rob the bank on June 27. They thought the vault would be stuffed with money because the town would be holding a big celebration for Civil War veterans. There would be a lot of drinking and merrymaking, and the outlaws hoped the town collectively would have its guard down as a result.

The bandits included Kid Curry, Sundance, Flat Nose Curry, Walt Punteney, and Tom O'Day. They camped out of town on June 26. Tom O'Day was assigned to go into town to look over the place. O'Day couldn't resist the watering holes and the party going on. He forgot about the job at hand and spent that day and the following night getting liquored up with the locals. He finally staggered back to camp with a hangover—it was now too late to pull the job that day. Worse, O'Day had forgotten to collect the information they needed. He did report that the jail had burned down.

They planned to hit the bank the next day.

O'Day again went ahead of the group to look things over, but he never got past the first bar. Rumor has it he tucked two whisky bottles into his saddlebags and drank them before the others rode in.

The bank job was a disaster, and the take was very disappointing. They bungled the holdup, but they managed to escape, barely.

Sundance, the Currys, and Punteney were taken prisoner following a shootout in Montana. They were brought back to Deadwood and jailed (since the jail in Belle Fourche had burned down). Tom O'Day was jailed too. Not being able to pass up a whiskey bottle, he had been captured rather quickly. The bail for the outlaws was ten thousand dollars.

John Mansfield was the jailer at the time. He was feeding the prisoners about eight o'clock one evening when Sundance jumped up and knocked the wind out of the surprised jailer with a few well-timed punches to the gut. Kid Curry and Sundance let out O'Day and Punteney. They escaped into the night.

Saddle horses were waiting for the men. Legend has it that Butch Cassidy and a few friends were there to help. It would be the kind of thing Butch would have done for a pal, but there is no evidence to prove this theory. Certainly someone had left the horses there, but perhaps it was just a lucky break. O'Day and Punteney were captured within the week. Kid Curry, Flat Nose, and Sundance made tracks. The object was to get as far from Deadwood as they could. Sundance headed south to meet up with Butch and Elza Lay. He wanted to be a long way from this part of the world—it held bad memories.

Likely at this time he began to realize that he wasn't a rocket scientist when it came to planning a job—and neither was Kid Curry. He did pull another job with Curry, but that was a few years later in Elko, Nevada. On one of his long vacations, Sundance went to Elko to gamble, a favorite pastime. The cards weren't turning well after a week or two, so before he left, he decided to even things up. In the wee hours, Sundance, Kid Curry, and Flat Nose Curry entered the Club Saloon and forced the

Below appear the photographs, descriptions and histories of GEORGE PARKER, alias "BUTCH" CASSIDY, alias GEORGE CASSIDY, alias INGERFIELD and HARRY LONGBAUGH alias HARRY ALONZO.

GEORGE PARKER.
First photograph taken July 15, 1894.

GEORGE PARKER.
Last photograph taken Nov. 21, 1900.

Name....George Parker, alias "Butch" Cassidy, alias George Cassidy, alias Ingerfield.
Nationality.....................American
Occupation................Cowboy; rustler
Criminal Occupation.....Bank robber and highwayman, cattle and horse thief
Age..36 yrs. (1901)..Height....5 feet 9 in
Weight..165 lbs...Build........Medium
Complexion..Light..Color of Hair.Flaxen
Eyes.....Blue......Mustache.Sandy, if any
Remarks:—Two cut scars back of head, small scar under left eye, small brown mole calf of leg. "Butch" Cassidy is known as a criminal principally in Wyoming, Utah, Idaho, Colorado and Nevada and has served time in Wyoming State penitentiary at Laramie for grand larceny, but was pardoned January 19th, 1896.

HARRY LONGBAUGH.
Photograph taken Nov. 21, 1900.

Name...........Harry Longbaugh, alias "Kid" Longbaugh, alias Harry Alonzo alias Frank Jones, alias Frank Boyd, alias the "Sundance Kid"
Nationality.......Swedish-American..Occupation.............Cowboy; rustler
Criminal Occupation.........Highwayman, bank burglar, cattle and horse thief
Age........35 years..............Height..................5 feet 10 in
Weight....165 to 175 lbs..............Build.......................Good
Eyes.....Blue or gray.............Complexion................Medium
Mustache or Beard.................(if any), natural color brown, reddish tinge
Features....Grecian type............Nose...................Rather long
Color of Hair..........Natural color brown, may be dyed; combs it pompadour.
IS BOW-LEGGED AND HIS FEET FAR APART.
Remarks:—Harry Longbaugh served 18 months in jail at Sundance, Cook Co., Wyoming, when a boy, for horse stealing. In December, 1892, Harry Longbaugh, Bill Madden and Henry Bass "held up" a Great Northern train at Malta, Montana. Bass and Madden were tried for this crime, convicted and sentenced to 10 and 14 years respectively; Longbaugh escaped and since has been a fugitive. June 28, 1897, under the name of Frank Jones, Longbaugh participated with Harvey Logan, alias Curry, Tom Day and Walter Putney, in the Belle Fourche, South Dakota, bank robbery. All were arrested, but Longbaugh and Harvey Logan escaped from jail at Deadwood, October 31, the same year. Longbaugh has not since been arrested.

We also publish below a photograph, history and description of CAMILLA HANKS, alias O. C. HANKS, alias CHARLEY JONES, alias "DEAF" CHARLEY, who may be found in the company of either PARKER, alias CASSIDY or LONGBAUGH, alias ALONZO, and for whom a proportionate amount of a $5,000.00 Reward is offered by the GREAT NORTHERN EXPRESS COMPANY upon arrest and conviction for participation in the Great Northern (Railway) Express robbery near Wagner, Mont., July 3rd, 1901.

Name...O. C. Hanks, alias Camilla Hanks, alias Charley Jones, alias Deaf Charley
Nationality.......American...........Occupation.....................Cowboy
Criminal Occupation............................Train robber; an ex-convict
Age..........38 years (1901)........Height...................5 feet 10 in
Weight....156 lbs................Build......................Good
Complexion.....Sandy...........Color of Hair..............Auburn
Eyes.....Blue.........Mustache or Beard......(if any), natural color sandy
Remarks:—Scar from burn, size 25c piece, on right forearm. Small scar right leg, above ankle. Mole near right nipple. Leans his head slightly to the left. Somewhat deaf. Raised at Yorktown, Texas; fugitive from there charged with rape; also wanted in New Mexico on charge of murder. Arrested in Teton County, Montana, 1892, and sentenced to 10 years in the penitentiary at Deer Lodge, for holding up Northern Pacific train near Big Timber, Montana. Released April 30th, 1901.

CAMILLA HANKS.
Photograph taken 1892.

HARVEY LOGAN, alias "KID" CURRY, referred to in our first circular issued from Denver on May 15, 1901, is now under arrest at Knoxville, Tenn., charged with shooting two police officers who were attempting his arrest.

BEN KILPATRICK, alias JOHN ARNOLD, alias "THE TALL TEXAN" of Concho County, Texas, another member of the Harvey Logan band of outlaws, engaged in the hold up, Mont., on November 6th, 1901, tried, convicted and sentenced to 10 years imprisonment for participation in the robbery of the GREAT NORTHERN EXPRESS COMPANY near Wagner, Mont.

WILLIAM CARVER, alias "BILL" CARVER, of Sonora, Sutton County, Texas, another member of this band, was killed at Sonora, Texas, April 2nd, 1901, by Sheriff E. S. Bryant, while resisting arrest on charge of murder.

IN CASE OF AN ARREST immediately notify PINKERTON'S NATIONAL DETECTIVE AGENCY at the nearest of the above listed offices.

Or
JOHN C. FRASER,
Resident Sup't., DENVER, COLO.

Pinkerton's National Detective Agency,
Opera House Block, Denver, Colo.

...requested to give this circular to the police of their city or district.
Police official, Marshal, Constable, Sheriff or Deputy, or a Peace officer.

Pinkertons Wanted poster featuring Butch Cassidy, the Sundance Kid, and Camilla Hanks

Pinkerton Archives

proprietor to open the safe at gunpoint. The robbers got between five hundred and three thousand dollars, probably not enough to break even, but enough for them to get back to Utah.

Within a few weeks, they were back in Brown's Hole. They knew that Butch was planning some big jobs, and they wanted to be a part of the action.

It was after Elza Lay went to prison in 1899 that Butch and Sundance became close friends. Sundance became a trusted second in command. He was obviously a quick study and tried not to make the same mistakes twice. It is generally understood that it was on the Wild Bunch's Tipton train robbery in 1900 that he first took Elza's place.

It's important to note that like Butch and many of the other Wild Bunch riders, the Sundance Kid was a criminal. He threatened deadly force to get money—stealing from people was his occupation. He could have been a fine rancher, but he was too busy taking shortcuts. He liked to drink, although he was rarely drunk. He liked to gamble, and he probably gambled too much. He enjoyed women of the evening. Nevertheless, he wasn't a mean-spirited man, and he had a number of good qualities. He was faithful to his friends, and he was charitable.

As with his partner in crime, Butch Cassidy, the evidence is conclusive that the Sundance Kid was not killed in San Vicente, Bolivia. (DNA tests on the bodies in question proved negative in 1995.) Their reported Bolivian death was surely a smoke screen to cover their tracks on both hemispheres, so they could slide into obscurity.

A number of people visited with Sundance after his return to the United States, including Matt Warner, the Bassett sisters, Butch, and Elza Lay. Calling himself Caleb Landreth, Sundance helped Elza look for the lost Caleb Rhoades Mines on Ute Indian land. Like Butch, Sundance Kid likely lived to a ripe old age.

Robber's Roost
The Outlaws' No-Man's-Land

Two men, Blue John and Silvertip, were supposedly the first to discover Robber's Roost and identify it as an ideal place to keep stolen livestock. They were mostly horse thieves and didn't want to be bothered by cattle.

Blue John (whose real name was John Griffith) had split eyes, one was blue and the other brown. He picked up the handle Blue because his single azure eye was a deep color and was the first thing anyone noticed about him. He was probably from England and spoke with a thick, lower-class British accent. He had only one set of clothes, and they were threadbare. His blue eye dropped a bit, giving him a droopy look, and he always needed a bath.

Silvertip (whose real name was James Howells) was brought up in the Smoky Mountains in Tennessee. He had a grizzle to his beard that reminded folks of a silvertip grizzly, which is how he got his nickname. Legend has it that the two raised quite a fuss in Moab, Utah, and got the law down on their backs. The sheriff was coming up fast when they slipped into the region that would later be known as Robber's Roost. They lost the law in the maze of canyons. Old Blue liked the area so well that he built a cabin near a spring. He took his time and built his house out of the only wood in the area, mountain cedar. His place became known as Blue John's Cabin. The spring is still known as Blue John's Spring.

Before the Wild Bunch was learning which end of a shooting iron to grab, another outlaw named Cap Brown was also using the Roost as a place to hold over his stolen livestock. Cap was an expert horse thief, and no herd in the territory in the 1870s was safe from his clever hand. He built corrals in a place he coined Twin Corral Flats. His operation was simple and lucrative. He stole livestock in Utah and took them to Colorado. The mines were especially eager to buy all the animals he could provide. Cap was very good, maybe one of the best horse thieves in the history of Utah. But it dawned on him that he could get a lot richer if he franchised his operation.

Cap rarely robbed from poor stock owners, since he needed their goodwill. He often employed the cash-starved ranchers to hold his stock for a few days or help him push the stolen herds toward the Roost. For their efforts, Brown paid the ranchers cash money, something that was hard to come by. He also collected eager, aspiring outlaws—boys mostly in their late teens—to help him. He organized them into bands and had them steal horses and drive them toward his stronghold. It was from Cap Brown that the young outlaw Mike Cassidy, Butch Cassidy's mentor, probably got his start in the rustling game.

Robber's Roost was a perfect haunt for outlaws. Lawmen never learned where the watering spots were. Outlaws would lead the posses pursuing them back and forth until the ragged lawmen were out of water—and often in a box canyon—then slip off. More than one man's bones bleached in the canyon's sun. Most turned back for town before it was too late.

The actual Roost was a 5-mile flat with lots of lookout points—although the entire area is referred to as Robber's Roost. The land held water, grass, and caves for shelter. Hanksville was 40 miles to the west on the Angel Trail. The town of Green River was nearly 50 miles to the north. Dandy Crossing was 25 miles to the south via Horseshoe Canyon or the Maze, from which a man could easily slip down to Mexico or over to Texas or New Mexico. The Henry Mountains were to the west (if a rustler shook off the law and needed to fatten up his beef before driving them to market).

Utah was different from its surrounding neighbors. There were fewer cattle barons. The land around the Roost (including Hanksville and Green River), for example, was dotted with small cattle ranches. Since the best farmland—land that could be irrigated—had been previously taken, later Mormon converts were assigned cattle ranches on the more arid land. Cattle did well on the desert plains, but it sometimes took between twenty-five and fifty acres per cow to make it pay. There was rustling, but nothing like the rustling that took place in Colorado, Wyoming, and Arizona, where large herds were taken at one time. Utah rustling was done a little bit differently.

Certainly, there were some wild cattle roaming the territory by the latter part of the nineteenth century. With the number of rugged canyons and arroyos on the vast plateau, wild cow hunting was a good business. There were also a number of "stray" mavericks near traditional rangelands that a rustler might find and brand—if he felt brave. And then, of course, there were the branded cattle—also potential targets for the courageous rustler.

In Utah, more often than not, a rustler took a handful of cattle and hoped his efforts wouldn't be spotted for a while—wholesale theft being somewhat uncommon since the outfits were small, and ranchers could keep closer tabs on their animals. Some ranchers did a little bit of rustling themselves. Many ranchers, even the honest ones, were hired to help push herds toward the Roost, knowing full well there wasn't a bill of sale for some of the cattle.

Rustlers would go on a sweeping raid of a region, taking a few cattle from a number of outfits until they had a herd built up. The advantage was that they didn't come anywhere near wiping out anyone, so they weren't as likely to be trailed. A man might be mad that he'd lost a few head, but it wasn't cost effective to spend a week or two trying to get his animals back. On their way to the Roost, the rustlers would take wild animals and mavericks as they found them.

The cattle were pushed into the Roost from as far away as the Sevier River Valley or the Wasatch Front. There was little chance of being followed if they moved fast and were careful. In Robber's Roost, brands might be added or altered while things cooled off. The land was very open, so while the feed wasn't really good, the cattle could range far and wide, and the outlaws knew where the water was. The cattle might be moved to another range (such as the Henry Mountains) to be fattened up. After a time, the herd would be pushed to market. Depending on where they were taken, this might be Green River or Price, but more likely somewhere in Colorado, often Telluride, or Wyoming.

After a robbery, the Wild Bunch often cooled off in Robber's Roost. The area was wild and desolate, but the Bunchers didn't go without their creature comforts. Instead of living in one of the many caves in the canyons, these outlaws enjoyed living in large canvas tents. They brought in many wagonloads of food and drink. Different women visited the camps. Some were prostitutes; others were wives or serious steadies. Etta Place, perhaps one or both of the Bassett sisters, and Maud Davis (wife of Elza Lay) were permanently attached to the Wild Bunch. There were other women who were not so discriminate—or very attractive. Their love-starved cliental didn't seem to mind. Two such women were Millie Nelson and Ella Butler. While Butch Cassidy didn't seem to mind steadies in camp, married or not, he was a little uncomfortable with the common trollop. Interestingly enough, Laura Bullion, who eventually rode with the Bunch on an outlaw raid in Wyoming and later paired up with different members of the gang, started out as a camp follower for hire before becoming a steady.

As a rule, Butch felt these ladies of easy virtue were prone to cause trouble and not to be trusted. Nevertheless, Millie and Ella (and Laura, too, for that matter) proved to be quite handy—in more ways than one. When the heat was on the bandit raiders, it was best to have the women slip into Green River, Price, or Hanksville and bring back supplies. While the outlaws were holding over in the Roost, Butch wanted his troops to keep sharp. And that meant polishing their marksmanship skills. On one occasion, the two women bought nearly nine hundred pounds of rifle and pistol rounds, along with such other essentials as flour, beans, and whiskey.

By the 1890s, the Roost was being used mostly by cattle thieves. However, when this stretch of land was first employed as a holdover zone, it held horses (cattle came later). Besides members of the Wild Bunch, a number of colorful outlaws called the Roost home. W. C. and Sam Snow were about as low and scummy as brothers could get. They didn't rob, they didn't murder, and they didn't steal. Coming from Utah County, they probably didn't even cuss. But they were sheep ranchers— the epitome of "white trash," according to cattle and horse ranchers. They pushed their flock of "range maggots" south to the Roost. The folks in that region were pretty tolerant about a man's lifestyle, but a sheepherder could not be tolerated. The brothers were given a day to get off the plain, or they'd be strung up and their sheep shot. In that day most ranches had a few sheep about the place for wool, but a flock was out of the question. Sheep ruined good grazing land by eating the grass all the way to the roots.

Jack Cottrell was a first-rate cattle thief, originally from Texas, and a lousy human being. No one ever said a good thing about him. Morality aside, he might have been one of the best rustlers in the region. Cottrell coveted his neighbor's wife, Ella Moore. Jack Cottrell and Jack Moore would become bitter foes, and Moore promised to put a bullet in Cottrell on sight. Cottrell had a small place on Bull Creek. He finally married—at least the widow took his name—but her daughter turned up pregnant, and he took off and was never heard from again.

Jack Moore was a Texas man who had drifted north for his health. Rumor has it he barely made it out of town before a lynching posse caught up to him. He brought his common-law wife, Ella. They lived about 20 miles southeast of Hanksville, staying with an Englishman named Buhr who had a nice ranch. Jack helped run the place, doing some serious rustling on the side, while Ella took care of the household.

Robber's Roost hasn't changed much in the last 150 years. It's still wild, desolate, and rugged. The land holds the spirits of those who formerly called this place home, including Gunplay Maxwell, Joe Walker, Flat Nose Curry, Kid Curry, Butch Cassidy, the Sundance Kid, Matt Warner, Mike Cassidy, Tom McCarty and brothers, Tom Dilly, and Cap Brown.

Elza Lay
The Brains behind Butch?

His real name was William Ellsworth. In the final days of the Old West, he was known as Elza Lay, the quiet outlaw in the famed Wild Bunch.

The name Elza (sometimes Elzy) came from shortening the first part of Ellsworth. Like many members of the Bunch, he used aliases as the occasion demanded. Most notably, he also went by William H. McGinnis (the name he used when he was incarcerated).

William Ellsworth was born in Ohio in 1868. He must have been brought up in a family that valued education. He surely attended school and was a promising student. He may have been carefully tutored at home, too. He was considered well educated by all who knew him. But more importantly, he had a great intellectual curiosity. He was rarely without a book in his saddlebags, and he read by firelight. He had a life-long love of learning and enjoyed reading and discussions. Like a number of men who rode the range, he was a "saddle academic" with an insatiable interest in history, literature, and the world around him. He was also a top ranch hand and handy with his Colt.

He had been a Texas cowboy for some time and had spent at least a few years in the Lone Star State. He probably migrated north from Texas with a cattle herd. He liked the Rocky Mountains so he stayed.

After leaving the cattle herd, he settled in Wyoming and found work on the Calvert Ranch near Baggs. Baggs was a favorite drinking town for outlaws and rustlers. Elza made a lot of connections with the locals on this part of the range. He was well liked and respected. Like Butch

Cassidy, he didn't often drink to excess, but he did like to drink. He no doubt found himself tilting an elbow with a fast crowd. He may have met some of his future partners in crime here. (A number of years later, after he got out of prison, he came back to the Baggs area—a place he thought of as home—and married one of the Calvert girls and raised a few children.) When he was on the run, some of these ranch folk were more than willing to help him slip away from the law and to provide a grubstake, a few bucks, a bag of cartridges, and a fresh horse.

After a while Elza left Baggs and moved west to Brown's Hole. He was a ranch hand at Matt Warner's place on Diamond Mountain. The young cowboy was good with horses and proved to be a tireless hand. He'd come well recommended from Charlie Crouse, a Brown's Hole rancher who had previously employed him to break horses. If he didn't meet Butch for the first time here at Warner's ranch, it was probably here that the two became fast friends. Before long the 6-foot-tall youngster was about to make a serious career change. Elza was good with a gun, excellent with stock, and quite intelligent. Most importantly, he was eager for some adventure. Butch had recruited quite a package.

Elza liked ranch life, but he liked the good life, too, which was hard to come by on a cowboy's salary. Before he got hooked up with the Wild Bunch, Elza would occasionally hang around the gambling strip near Fort Duchesne or visit the saloons in Vernal, Utah. He'd head back to the Hole when he'd lost his wad. He could afford a night or two with the roulette wheels spinning and the poker games humming every month or so—but that was it. A cowhand's wages went only so far. Once in a while he'd get into a minor scrape, but he was no different from most cowhands. He'd fight if pushed, but he wasn't the sort who looked for trouble. He'd rather avoid it. Other than some rustling, which was a given with his current employer, he kept his nose clean.

He committed his first serious crime in August 1896. He jumped from being a happy-go-lucky cowboy who did a little bit of moonlight

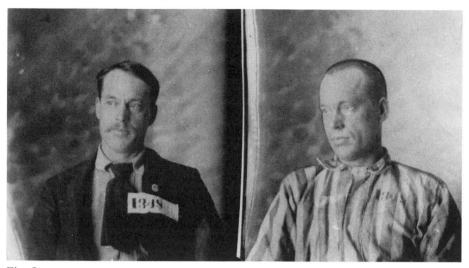

Elza Lay

rustling to being a wanted criminal with a major price tag on his head. He was a key player in the Montpelier, Idaho, bank robbery.

There was no going back. If the West hadn't known his handle before, it would now. He was about to become one of the most influential criminals in the West—the quiet lieutenant of Butch Cassidy. He was the man behind the scenes. He had no problem with his friend taking center stage.

Along with his new friend Butch and a group soon to be called the Wild Bunch, Elza helped steal $7,100 at Colt-point. The young Elza might have justified his crime, at least to himself. The reason for the job was not selfish. Rather, it was to get money to pay for Matt Warner's legal defense. Matt had managed to get himself captured and was rotting in a Wyoming jail. Elza thought a lot of Matt and considered him one of his best friends. Probably he figured the job was more a favor to Matt than an actual crime. Maybe he didn't think about it much at all. The entire caper could have been a youthful impetuous reaction. It's likely he wasn't thinking of himself as a criminal yet—even after the robbery. The outlaws turned the money over to Douglas Preston, a lawyer from Rock Springs, Wyoming, so he could work on Matt's defense.

Nevertheless, an Idaho posse was close on the bandits' heels. There were some touchy moments, but the bandits effected an escape. Favor or not to Matt, those weren't blanks the men in the posse had loaded in their Colts and Winchesters. It might have been more thrilling than terrifying. It didn't matter now if outlawing was in Elza's blood or not—he was branded as a serious criminal.

Like Butch, Elza was liked by nearly everyone who met him. He got along admirably with the local ranchers and homesteaders. The loose collection of outlaws around the Hole liked him and, more importantly, respected his judgment and didn't feel threatened by his decisions. Elza must have been a good judge of character to keep the likes of Kid Curry and a few other of his volatile cohorts with short fuses from going off. He had the ability to think clearly and quickly and was a careful planner. When Butch Cassidy and Elza Lay rode together, they were arguably the two finest outlaw minds in the West. Like Butch, Elza saw no reason to take stupid chances or to be unnecessarily violent. If there were ever two western soul mates, it was these two partners in crime.

Elza, in today's language, would be called laid-back and unpretentious. At one point in the early days, many of the outlaws considered him the natural, informal leader of the Wild Bunch. The Bassett family had nothing but praise for him—and both Ann and her sister, Josie, could be sharp-tongued when describing folks. They called him the "educated member of the Wild Bunch," a real gentleman.

Elza's most famous robbery in Utah was the Castle Gate payroll job. His last job with the Bunch was probably the Wilcox, Wyoming, holdup in June 1899. A month later, while on a Wild Bunch hiatus, he hooked up with the Black Jack Ketchum Gang. Two back-to-back jobs were out of character for him. Perhaps he was trying to make one last score so he could reconcile with his estranged wife, Maud. They had a great deal of conflict over his line of work. She wanted him to settle down, hopefully in Utah. When they had first married, he wasn't ready to leave the outlaw trail, but by now it had become old. Elza, like the others, could tell that the law was closing in. If he didn't retire soon, it was only a matter of time before he would be caught.

Black Jack Ketchum invited Elza to ride with him for a big score. Ketchum didn't ask Butch or Sundance, since he knew they'd say no. Neither Butch nor Sundance trusted Black Jack's professional judgment. They thought his jobs were sloppy. Besides, he and his boys were indiscriminate with their six-guns. Both Butch and Sundance tried to talk Elza out of riding with Black Jack. They thought it was a formula for disaster. The usually cautious Elza committed perhaps the biggest error in judgment of his professional career, and it would cost him dearly.

The Ketchum Gang, accompanied by Elza, robbed a train. The job wasn't well planned by Elza's usual standards. Almost at once, a large posse was after the bandits. At a camp on Turkey Creek, the posse overtook the outlaws and a serious gunfight ensued. The sheriff and several others were killed. The outlaws split up and a wounded Elza managed to escape. He was later captured in Eddy County, New Mexico, and charged with killing the sheriff, which he claimed he didn't do. He was also charged with interfering with the U.S. mail. Elza was tried and given a life sentence in the Santa Fe prison. While he was in the pen, his wife, Maud, decided she'd had enough and divorced him.

Elza was a model inmate who became the warden's pet, for lack of a better term. He must have had some influence with the prisoners, too, since he helped stop a prison riot. Things started to look good for the man who had been given life in the pen. The warden worked on getting this promising young man a pardon or at least an early parole. The fact that the chief prison officer was interested in gold mining didn't hurt Elza's chances. Elza hinted that he knew some likely places to look for gold mines on Ute Indian land in Utah. He further hinted that they might get rich if he wasn't locked up. There was plenty of gold. Elza suggested that he had worked for Caleb Rhodes, a famous miner, as a guard. The warden was a bit greedy, and the likable young man could see it. In the meantime, Elza got Matt Warner, who was now out of prison, to send him a "mystery" map of the area. This map only served to whet the warden's appetite—the man was almost ready to count his gold.

The warden's good friend, Miguel Otero, who happened to be the governor of New Mexico, was also interested in the project. The warden would work on getting Elza out of prison early while Otero worked on a pardon. The two officials became silent partners in the venture. They would form a company and put up the needed capital, while the young man, now completely "reformed," would be "pardoned" for a crime he probably hadn't committed anyway. Elza would provide the legwork while in the field. He'd search for the "lost" gold mine, find it, and make them all rich.

Around Christmas of 1905, Elza walked out of prison with some pocket money, more capital on the way, and a smile on his face. (He was officially pardoned a month later.) Gold mines, after all, wait for no man. He formed several mining companies, but nothing came of them.

Later, Elza drifted up to the Brown's Hole area and again went to work on the Calvert Ranch. Three years later he wedded Mary Calvert. After that, he ran the local saloon while he and his wife raised a pair of daughters. He also did a bit more gold mining. He moved from job to job, including wildcatting oil. The reformed family man had studied geology with a great intensity, and in the course of his wildcatting discovered the Hiawatha Oil Fields in Wyoming and some promising areas near Ogden, Utah. While he was good at finding oil, it was precarious business, and he finally went bust. He moved farther west and worked as a gambler and finally as a watermaster at Imperial Valley Irrigation in California.

After his prison stint he stayed straight. He visited his old friends who were alive—including Butch and Sundance. He died in 1934 from a heart attack as a respectable man.

——— Kid Curry ———
More Wanted than Butch and Sundance

His real name was Harvey Logan. In his day, Kid Curry was better known and more feared than Butch Cassidy or the Sundance Kid. Certainly, there was a higher price on his head. Because of his ruthlessness, some erroneously thought he was the real leader of the Wild Bunch.

He was born in 1865 in Tama, Iowa, into modest circumstances. He was orphaned and raised by his Aunt Lee in Missouri. At age nineteen, he went West to be a cowboy near Big Spring, Texas. He followed up the trail herds and later met up with his brothers where they ranched in Montana.

He picked up the name Kid when he was in Texas. He added the name Curry in honor of his good friend George (Flat Nose) Curry. Kid Curry started out as a decent sort and probably would have been a successful rancher, but he had a few unlucky breaks. He also had a hard time holding his temper. He was known as a good cowboy and a patient man with livestock. He was skilled at breaking raw horses and was loyal to his friends. He was well liked, but when he was drinking a sour mood possessed him. Those who knew him got out of his way. The Kid could be a violent man, even a cold-blooded murderer at times. But he must have had a good side, too. Butch Cassidy liked him and was able to keep his moods in check. Indeed, Butch may have been the only man who could do this consistently. On a number of jobs, Butch frequently kept Curry from squeezing the trigger. Curry, it seems, didn't mind the patient reproof. On the Wilcox job, Curry was all for plugging a man named

Harvey Logan in his Kid Curry persona
Union Pacific Railroad Archives

Woodcock who had refused to open the door. Curry wanted to shoot the man for his stubbornness, but Butch wouldn't let him. In spite of his faults, Curry was a core member of the Bunch. He was also personally invited to go to South America with Butch and Sundance.

There is little question that Curry not only respected Butch as a leader but also as a person. During the famous meeting at Cassidy Point at Brown's Hole, Butch wanted to organize the outlaws into the Train Robbers Syndicate and be their leader. During Butch's most important sales pitch, possibly to as many as two hundred outlaws, Curry jumped in and offered his services as leader, no doubt upsetting Butch's apple cart. Rather than fight about it with guns, as Curry usually seemed inclined to do, he took Butch's suggestion: Both prospective leaders led men on robberies to see who would be the most successful. Butch won hands down. Curry was a good outlaw and could execute a robbery, but he wasn't very good at long-range planning or escaping after the job.

After that, Curry didn't seem to mind being subordinate to Butch and accepted the fact willingly. He respected the man. It is assumed that Curry also had some leadership qualities, since Sundance followed him and not Butch after the meeting at Cassidy Point. It speaks well for Butch that he didn't hold a grudge and that Sundance, as well as Curry, later saw Butch as their effectual leader.

Curry's first scrape with the law came when he was still fairly young. He had pushed a herd up from the Cimarron into Pueblo. In a moment of relaxation, he got into a saloon brawl and someone got hurt. He had to leave town ahead of a posse.

For more than twenty years, Kid Curry would have a price on his head. Indeed, most of the murders committed by the Wild Bunch, and there weren't many, were committed by him. He spent a lot of time in Utah, but most of his crimes, except for the murder of two Utah lawmen, were committed in other states. Robber's Roost and Brown's Hole were his hiding spots.

He could have outridden his first few scrapes with the law (they were pretty minor). He tried to go straight several times—except for a bit of rustling on the side. He and his brothers had a good working ranch near Landusky, Montana, on Rock Creek. Curry had a drooping, light brown mustache that covered his lips. Some say this gave him an expressionless appearance, like a prairie rattler. He was of average height and not a bad-looking man. One would think he was a cowboy. However, he got involved in a killing that put him firmly over the line.

Pike Landusky was a founding father of the town and a man who commanded a lot of respect. He also had a pretty daughter that the local bucks, including the Curry brothers, liked to chase. A prospecting boom occurred near their ranch, and Pike got pretty heavy-handed with the Curry boys—he'd also been elected the sheriff of the town that bore his name.

Pike was feeling his oats at the local watering hole one day, and the Kid was a little under his whiskey. It so happened that Elfia, Pike's daughter, had gotten herself in the family way and had fingered the Kid for the father. She liked him and thought this was a good way to catch him. Truth be told, the Kid's brother was probably the father—at least he thought so. But Pike Landusky was a mean-spirited man and prodded Kid Curry, even insulting his dead mother. Pike roughed up the Kid pretty bad and arrested him. The Kid was unarmed, and Pike's friends greatly outnumbered him. He was put in jail. There was a five-hundred-dollar bond on his freedom.

Apparently, Pike worked his daughter over, too, for her poor judgment and for embarrassing the family. Some versions of the story say she had a miscarriage after the beating.

The Kid promised he'd get even. Friends put up the bond, and later he paid a fifty-dollar fine.

The two men met again soon in the saloon. With the odds more even, Kid Curry beat Pike Landusky to a bloody pulp. As Curry was walking away, Pike drew on the unarmed man. Some accounts say that

Pike shot first and missed. Others say that a friend named Thornhill loaned Curry his gun. At the local inquest, eleven witnesses said it was a fair fight. They all testified that Pike drew (and possibly shot) first. Yes, Kid Curry shot and killed the man, but it was in self-defense. Judge Debois was a friend of Pike Landusky's and known to be crooked. He was about to rule against Curry in spite of the evidence, so the Kid and his brothers took off. Curry wasn't about to stick around and get hung.

Now there was a serious price on his head. He had tried to make an honest living, and the system wouldn't let him. This experience soured him on criminal justice. He hated jails. In his career he would make two spectacular jailbreaks—one in Deadwood, South Dakota, in 1897 and the other in Knox County, Tennessee, in 1902. During the latter break, he made a lasso from pieces of wire he'd salvaged from some brooms. He lassoed a prison guard and tied him up with string he'd made from his clothing. Curry then stole the man's keys and sidearms and took him hostage until he could get to a horse and escape.

Curry didn't like lawmen, either. He left the bodies of sheriffs in Utah, Wyoming, and Arizona. He left the bodies of other men who tangled with him across the West. He was fast with his gun, a deadly shot, and he wasn't afraid to shoot first. It's not surprising that Kid Curry was one of the most wanted men in the country. Indeed, he was the most wanted member of the Wild Bunch.

Curry wasn't one to let a grudge go unresolved. In 1896, while riding with Black Jack Ketchum's band, the Curry brothers got in a serious scuffle with a rancher named Jim Winters. Apparently, the rancher had been spying on them, and, worse, he'd been talking trash. To avenge their honor, the brothers confronted him to shut him up. It is said that Winters was handy with a sawed-off 12-bore. In the ensuing gunfight, Johnny Curry was blown apart from a wicked blast. With Johnny dead and things closing in upon them, Kid and his other brothers took off. However, the young outlaw vowed he'd seek vengeance on the rancher for the murder of his little brother. In July 1901, with the law on his tail just after the Great Northern train robbery, Kid Curry slipped away from the posses, hunted down Jim Winters, and killed him. He felt the score was finally even, although it had taken six years.

Curry was either in Texas relaxing in his favorite "house of the rising sun" or in New Mexico (accounts differ) when he heard news that made him shiver. Lonnie (his last surviving brother) had been ruthlessly gunned down by a Missouri posse near his aunt's house. And the sheriff in Moab, Utah, had shot Flat Nose George Curry. Flat Nose was like family to the Kid. They weren't related, but he'd used Flat Nose's last name as his outlaw sobriquet to show him respect.

He couldn't do anything about the Missouri killing at the time, but he could go to Utah and hunt down Sheriff John Tyler and Deputy Sheriff Sam Jenkins and exact revenge.

He killed Tyler and Jenkins as retribution for his friend's death. How and where he did it is open to debate. No one seems to agree on the how—only that he did it. According to one account, the romantic account, he checked the loads in his six-gun, drank his last sip of cowboy coffee, and poured the pot on the sagebrush fire. Even though he was a wanted man, he boldly rode into the hot, desert town of Moab, Utah, and called the two men out to meet him in the street. In some sort of fair fight, he was able to outdraw and kill both men, riding away feeling vindicated. The murderers were 6 feet deep, and now Flat Nose could rest easy.

Another account says the law got wind that Kid Curry, the most wanted man in Utah, was in the mountains, biding his time, getting ready to hunt out the sheriffs who had killed his friend. Not wanting to wait, a large posse went out to find the wanted man with the help of Sheriff Preece and Moab Sheriff Tyler. The posse split up, and Tyler and Jenkins (who in some accounts was a posse member and not a deputy) rode together.

Tyler's group came upon fresh signs of a possible outlaw camp.

Pinkerton's Wanted poster featuring Harvey Logan, a.k.a Kid Curry
Pinkerton Archives

Tying up their horses, the posse snuck in. Tyler identified his group and told the outlaws to disarm. Kid Curry had vowed never to surrender, and he started to fire. For some reason, the lawmen may have turned to run for their horses, possibly to get their rifles. They ended up with bullets in their back. Other members of the posse escaped and found Preece's group. Preece rode for Thompson to get reinforcements before continuing the search. Curry (and friends) got away.

Still in a sour mood a few days later, Curry came upon the Norman brothers, whom he had known earlier. Some kind of violent argument ensued. Perhaps the Normans got greedy and thought of turning Curry in. Maybe there were bad feelings over a poker game. It could be that Curry was on the prod, and one of the brothers said something touchy. Colts soon did the talking, or rather Curry's Colt did the talking. Both brothers were found neatly shot, and Curry took credit for it.

It was a busy, bloody summer for Curry. He met up with the Bunch and participated in the Tipton job in which the gang got somewhere around fifty thousand dollars. To relax and hide out, Curry headed for Texas and his favorite whorehouse, Hell's Half Acre, and his favorite sporting woman, Annie.

After the Wild Bunch lost Butch and Sundance, a few successful jobs were pulled. However, Curry had problems formulating escape plans. While Butch was around, Curry followed Butch's plans and things went well. Now that Butch was gone, Curry had the stick-'em-up part right, but that was all.

Not only were posses and lawmen where they never had been before, the law was using modern techniques to catch outlaws. They could trace stolen money, which did Curry and the Tall Texan in. All the law had to do was wait for the outlaws to start spending the loot, and the lawmen knew where to go after them. Curry did some jail time.

On June 9, 1904, near Rifle, Colorado, Ben Kilpatrick (the Tall Texan), Charlie Howland, and Kid Curry hit a train. The take was small, and a posse was soon on their tail. A shootout occurred, and supposedly more than two hundred rounds were fired. Curry took a shot through his lungs and couldn't escape. He knew he was dying, so he told the others to flee while he kept the posse busy. He held off the posse until his friends got away.

Rather than be apprehended, Curry turned his well-worn Colt on himself.

——➤·◦·≺—— Wild Bunch Women ——➤·◦·≺——
Consorts, Wives, and Ladies of the Night

In many ways, the Wild Bunch women were as bold and dynamic as the men who kept them company. A great deal is written, for example, about Etta Place—the most famous companion. Nevertheless, we still don't know that much about her. There's understandably a great deal of speculation. The real Etta was, and is, an enigma. Etta Place probably wasn't even her real name. Few in the Wild Bunch, man or woman, used their given names, presumably so that one's family could be spared the shame of being related to an outlaw—or worse, a fallen woman.

There are a number of overlapping theories coupled with a plethora of conflicting data. Etta sightings, like Elvis sightings, have become quite fashionable. An entire group of historians have honed in on her, making the study of Etta Place their life's work.

Certainly, some theories are more convincing than others. Most everyone agrees that Etta Place was the Sundance Kid's partner (various accounts call her *wife, common-law wife, whore, consort, favorite lady of the evening, schoolteacher,* or *companion*). However, it's also fairly certain that she spent a considerable amount of time with Butch Cassidy first. After her relationship with Butch cooled, she played musical chairs, or beds as the case might be, with his good friend and partner—with no hard feelings on anyone's part. Elza Lay's daughter, when interviewed at a later date, suggested that it was common knowledge in her family that Etta was with Butch first—perhaps as early as the fall of 1896.

This is a credible observation since Butch rented a cabin near Vernal for Elza Lay and his new bride, Maud. Later on, blankets were hung across the middle for privacy, so Butch and his companion could occupy the other side. Butch's consort in this cozy arrangement was supposedly Etta Place.

Etta was extremely attractive and could probably easily steal a man's heart. An adjective often used to describe her is *striking*. She had wonderfully thick hair and intelligent, deep-brown eyes as well as an alluring smile, a calming voice, and a pleasant personality. She was on the small side, rather shapely, and quick-witted. At first glance, she seemed more likely to be the wife of a senator or a wealthy businessman—not the sort of woman who would be the sidekick of a notorious outlaw. Apparently Etta craved adventure and excitement, something Butch and Sundance could give her. She enjoyed spending her lover's unlawful gains. She was always well dressed and classy. She must have completely trusted her boys in crime—enough to uproot and take off for the wilds of South America with them. (Perhaps the thirty-five thousand dollars in cold cash they took for emergencies put some of her other anxieties to rest.)

Was she a lonely schoolmarm who felt trapped in her one-room classroom, as some historians have written? Was she bored with life and her profession? In an existential midlife crisis, did she hook up with two middle-aged Peter Pans and play the doting Wendy? Certainly her experience with schoolboys came in handy, as the outlaws often acted like overgrown schoolboys themselves. Either way, she was quite educated and refined, a woman of breeding, style, and culture.

Some scholars have suggested that Etta might have been Ann Bassett, the "Queen of the Rustlers" from Brown's Hole. Ann was definitely an off-on girlfriend of Butch for some time. Maybe she changed her name and had a few long outlaw flings. The fiery Ann would have liked and appreciated the wild life as a consort to the West's smartest bandits. While Ann was a feisty sort, she was also capable of being charming. Robbery and rustling wouldn't have bothered her. Ann and Etta shared many physical characteristics. Ann liked and understood outlaws, for she was barely housebroken herself.

The theory that Ann and Etta were the same woman gained credibility in the 1990s. Computer analysis of existing photos of Ann Bassett and Etta Place spotted curious similarities. Doris Burton and the Outlaw Trail Historical Association spearheaded this project. They sent pictures of each woman to the Computer Research Group at Los Alamos National Laboratories. Using enhanced scans to look at things the human eye can't see, initial tests apparently confirmed only a 1 in 5,000 chance that Etta and Ann were two different women. A further test showed a barely noticeable scar on Ann's forehead. Etta's photo is supposed to have the same scar, though it's not visible to the human eye. However, it was picked up by computer analysis.

Some historians have tried to corroborate the picture theory by comparing some of the dates Ann left her ranch and aligning them with the times Etta was known to be with Butch or Sundance. They suggest that in the fall of 1900, Ann left her home for a vacation; right after this, Etta showed up in Texas to visit Sundance. A short time later, in February 1901, Ann again left Brown's Hole. The *Vernal Express* wrote, "Miss Anne Bassett left Brown's Park on the stage for Texas." Ann was gone for quite some time. She had been "traveling abroad," the same paper reported when she returned not quite two years later. According to Pinkerton records, Etta, Butch, and Sundance returned to the United States from South America in July 1902. Before the end of the summer, the absent Ann was back at her ranch in Brown's Hole. Many reputable scholars are still not convinced that Ann was Etta Place—letters with postmarks indicate that Ann had vacationed in the United States and was not in South America. So the mystery still isn't solved.

Another theory of Etta's identity came from Frank Dimaio, a seasoned Pinkerton detective. He tailed the trio across South America and felt that Etta was originally one of the girls from Fanny Porter's Sporting House in the red-light district of San Antonio, Texas. He thought her real name might have been Laura Etta Place and that she was from Arizona. Her father had died suddenly, and she was left destitute and in desperate circumstances. She ended up as a reluctant working girl in a house of sin. Butch found her and rescued her from that sordid life, sending her to Price to live with a respectable Mormon family named Thayne. There she taught school and carried on a relationship with the two most famous Wild Bunchers. This wouldn't have been out of character for Butch. He bought railroad tickets and bankrolled several "soiled doves" who wanted to quit the business.

Another similar theory is that Etta was a hooker in Fort Worth who had come from the Midwest, probably Missouri. Her name was thought to be Eunice Gray, and she lived until 1962, when she died in a hotel fire. Other historians have connected Etta to the Parkers in Utah. They think she was one of Butch's (LeRoy Parker's) cousins, born in Kanosh, Utah, and raised near Joseph, Utah, not far from Butch's childhood home. She and Butch knew each other as children and got reacquainted as adults.

Others have suggested that Etta acquired the name Place when she started traveling with Kid Curry. His mother's maiden name was Annie Place. On some occasions, Etta signed her name Ethel, which may have been her real name. Her last name might have been Thayne. On a trip back to the United States in 1902, the pair registered on the British ship *Honorius* as Mr. and Mrs. Harry Place.

In New York, before heading to South America, she was treated like royalty. One of her gifts was a gold watch from Tiffany's. Along with the Sundance Kid, she posed for the now-famous photograph at DeYoung's Studio on Broadway. By 1907 Etta slips out of western historical legend into western enigma. One theory says that she had appendicitis and came back to the States for an operation at a Denver hospital. Reportedly, Sundance checked her in and walked away, never to return. Strangely, there's no record in any hospital of a patient who fits her description. Some say she died in Colorado.

Laura Bullion (alias Della Rose, Laura Casey, Clare Hayes) was a pretty girl, with a good figure and a way with men. She may have had slightly bucked teeth.

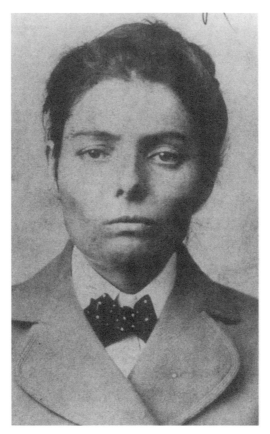

Laura Bullion
Pinkerton Archives

Laura was probably born in Kentucky in 1873 and raised in Texas. When she met up with the Wild Bunch, she was likely working in Sheridan, Wyoming, in a dance hall. She'd been on her own from an early age and was somewhat hardened.

A reporter who interviewed her before her trial said, "She [could] talk like a machine gun" if she wanted to. Of course, at the time the journalist recorded this, she'd just been arrested for a serious crime and was probably nervous. Apparently, she always chewed gum, leading some to assume she had an anxious personality. However, others said she could be soft-spoken and calm. She may have serviced a number of the Wild Bunch in the early days, being a camp follower as a matter of survival.

She liked the wild life, being outdoors, and being out of the smoky dance halls. She also liked the security of being with one man. Her first serious steady was probably Will Carver. This pairing may have happened as early as 1896. A few years later, she shifted her affections to the Tall Texan (Ben Kilpatrick), who became the true love of her life. She was taken aback by the Tall Texan's good looks and pleasant manner. By then, Carver's affections had shifted to a prostitute named Lillie.

Some think Laura had known the Tall Texan as a child back in Texas. At some point, she became the Tall Texan's common-law wife, striving to be true as long as it was convenient—and the money held out. She is the only woman who actually took part in the Wild Bunch's raids, including the infamous Tipton train robbery in Wyoming.

In 1901 the Tall Texan participated in a robbery with some former colleagues at Wagner, Montana. Laura helped. After the caper, the two star-crossed lovers headed east to celebrate under the names of Mr. and Mrs. Benjamin Arnold. The party didn't last long. They left a literal paper trail of hot notes and were captured within a few days. Laura, now twenty-eight years old, was sentenced to five years. She always maintained that she was innocent. Upon release, she possibly opened a boardinghouse. Some say she waited for her lover, but he never showed up. After he was released from prison, he was promptly shot in 1912 while robbing a train.

Annie Rogers (alias Maud Williams) worked in the red-light district in a Texas bordello. She was a favorite and sometime traveling companion of Kid Curry. At one time, Annie, along with her good friend Lillie Davis, another working professional, went on a long vacation with Kid Curry and Will Carver. The four traveled to the state fair, ate ice cream, and then rode the train north for a long, luxurious holiday so they could spend all that hard-earned stolen money.

Annie Rogers and Harvey Logan (Kid Curry)
Pinkerton Archives

Lillie wanted to be "respectable," so she talked Will into marrying her, probably in Denver. They stayed in the finest hotels. The two women were showered with expensive clothes in the best French fashions. The outlaws wore expensive suits (with six-guns smartly tucked into their waistbands). They drank imported wines and ate in four-star restaurants.

Occasionally, the two outlaws left the girls to pull a job—no doubt needing a refill in the cash department since this vacation was very expensive. Curiously, Annie had Kid Curry order some very expensive sets of silk underwear. (Curry was very proud of his fancy drawers.)

After the train job in Tipton, Curry called for Annie again. He said he had bags of money—which were quickly spent. This wild party went off and on for some time.

By 1901 Curry was in jail. He was caught with the goods from the Wagner robbery. Annie, who had enjoyed the wild ride, knew the game was over. Worse, she was implicated in the robbery, too. In his own way, Curry probably had more affection for Annie than any other woman he'd known. He loved her, and she loved him. But both were pragmatic about their lifestyles and their relationship.

Curry told authorities that Annie had not been involved in the last caper, and she was acquitted. He told her to cooperate with the law so she could stay out of prison. With Curry's blessing, Annie talked—basically telling the authorities what they already knew. She wouldn't do jail time.

She wished Curry well in their last visit and returned to Texas. She may have sold the big diamond Curry had given her and possibly quit the life of a sporting woman. She may have returned to Illinois, where she dropped out of recorded history.

Josie and Ann Bassett were a handful. The West never bred a more colorful pair. The sisters had the men of Brown's Hole wrapped about their little fingers. Each was strong-willed and seemed to have a volatile temper (Ann's was more mercurial), but each could be charming and seductive, too, if not downright manipulative. The two had the innocence of a schoolgirl blended with a streetwalker's savvy. They were combinations of Mother Teresa, Mata Hari, and Lady Macbeth. They lived when the West was wild and woolly, when the open range stretched ahead for days without a fence.

Like their mother, Elizabeth, either sister would help a neighbor in need—even with rustled beef. And like their mother, they'd grub-staked many a drifter. Their riders were fiercely loyal to them. Both girls were crack shots and expert horsewomen, and they could roll their own cigarettes (in a day when women usually didn't smoke).

They also "got around." Each was married a handful of times and had a string of lovers. They fit the profile of the current sexual revolution more completely than the closing days of Victorianism allowed. Saint Mary's in Salt Lake or Miss Potter's School couldn't break the spirit of these western mustangs.

Both lived long enough to see the jet age, two world wars, and the horrific destruction of nuclear weapons. Ann died in May 1956 at age seventy-eight. Josie spent her last fifty years at Cub Creek, now in Dinosaur National Monument, without electricity or running water. She died in 1964 at age eighty-nine.

Butch Cassidy came to the Bassett Ranch in 1889 to escape from a posse. He was a good-looking, likeable young outlaw, the kind of man who could take a young woman's heart without meaning to. He laid low at the Bassett Ranch after his first major robbery in Telluride, Colorado. Josie, who was born in 1874, was in full bloom and certainly would have attracted the eye of the young outlaw. She often referred to him as her "Brown Park beau." They went to dances and soon became an item.

Butch spent a lot of time reading in Herb Bassett's library. Both Josie and Ann had been well educated and had been to finishing schools. A man who was strong and bold, yet sensitive enough to read good literature, was surely an attractive fellow. He could handle himself in a frontier gunfight or fistfight, he could rustle and brand a stolen steer with ease, but he could also talk with authority about the Lake Poets and had read Scott, Tennyson, and Austen.

Butch and Elza Lay were very grateful to the Bassett family—or so the legend goes in Ann's account (she had a tendency to tell some stretchers, and one has to take her stories with a grain of salt). To show their appreciation, the outlaws put on a Thanksgiving Day feast. In her memoirs, Ann recalled that this day was not soon forgotten among the locals. The outlaws, dressed in dark suits, white shirts, stiff collars, and bowties, served the food. There was roast turkey, chestnut dressing, giblet gravy, cranberry sauce, biscuits, mashed potatoes, sweet potatoes, pumpkin pies, and plum pudding. Everyone dressed up. Ann suggests that Butch was better as a gunman than as a waiter, and she and Josie teased him all night about it.

Josie tells about her first meeting with Butch, who was known as George Cassidy in those days. There had been a horse race at the Crouse ranch on the north side of the Green River. It was a long, straight track, unlike the oval ones of modern times. The horses raced to one end, abruptly turned around, and spurred back to the finishing line. It was an exciting event. Folks from all over Brown's Hole came to see the fun, bringing picnics. Whiskey flowed, and later there was a barn dance.

Cassidy, rode one of Crouse's favorite horses. "I thought he was the most dashing and handsome man I ever seen," Josie recalled. "I was such a young thing . . . and looked upon Butch as my knight in shining armor. He was more interested in his horse than he was in me, and I remember being very put off by that. I went home after being snubbed by him and stamped my foot in frustration."

Josie admits in this account that she and Butch were lovers, but she doesn't define the term. Apparently, one time some men were after Butch, and he hid in the Bassett barn. He read books from the library, but he couldn't read by lantern at night because of the danger of fire. He told Josie he'd be bored up there all by himself. Josie recalled, "Well, all I can say is, I didn't let him get bored."

The love affair may have been rekindled off and on as a romance of convenience. Butch was gone a good bit of the time, and Josie wasn't one to sit home alone. Josie apparently met Butch between jobs. She said they rendezvoused at towns in Nevada and Wyoming on weekends. Butch and Josie remained good friends. Josie claims she saw Butch as late as the 1920s and that her sister, Ann, had seen him from time to time, too.

Josie had spent time with Elza Lay in the early 1890s. He worked for the Bassetts off and on. Josie always referred to Elza as "the finest gentleman I've ever known." Elza and Josie went to dances together and spent a lot of evenings talking. Elza's grandson suggested that Elza and Josie were lovers—although likely they were lovers with an "understanding" rather than passion. They were certainly fond of each other, but Elza's life wouldn't allow him to settle down.

Josie went through five husbands, divorcing four of them. Her first husband wasn't a good match, but she was quite pregnant when she said, "I do." He was the former Bassett ranch manager. Josie tended to be a lot more domestic than her sister. She liked the duties of being a ranch wife, and she enjoyed her children. She was fond of taking care of a kitchen garden, making soap, baking bread and cookies, keeping house, and helping with ranch chores.

She was widowed once. There were rumors of poison. She always said that if you can't get rid of a man one way, you get rid of him another. She chased off her last husband with a fry skillet—no doubt after bending it over his head. To make ends meet, Josie bootlegged whiskey, although she wasn't much of a drinker. She was accused of rustling cattle when she was sixty-two years old but was acquitted. She said she was framed, although a number of hides were found on her ranch.

Ann Bassett was born in Brown's Hole in 1878. She was the younger of the two Bassett sisters, often referred to as Queen of the Rustlers or Queen Ann. These were titles she enjoyed. She was a wild girl who loved the land she had been raised on. Indeed, the land itself was her truest love. While her sister didn't mind domestic household chores, Ann hated them. She wanted to be on horseback out on the range. As a thirteen-year-old girl, Ann made up her mind to rope a silvertip grizzly cub. She couldn't have been naive about the dangers. In her day, grizzlies still roamed the Hole with some frequency. She was simply stubborn. She did what she wanted without worrying about the consequences. She knew the dangers of messing with a temperamental bruin, but she didn't care. In this case, the mother bear had other ideas, like ripping her into pieces. The precocious girl managed to climb up a tree just in time. The enraged bear shook the aspen, hoping to loosen her from the branches. When that didn't happen, the sow took her anger out on Ann's horse, tearing it to shreds. The commotion caught the attention of some Bassett ranch hands. They shot the bear and rescued the girl.

She was the only Bassett child that her father, the gentle Herb, ever physically disciplined. When she was a young girl, her father told her not to play with an ax. He'd been barking some logs and was taking a break. She told him she wanted to peep the logs, too, just like a man. This was a dangerous job, and a child who didn't know what she was doing could seriously hurt herself. He told her again to stop, and she flew off the handle, calling him a "son of a bitch" and telling him to leave her alone. This outburst resulted in a trip to the woodshed.

When her ranch was threatened by cattle barons, Ann lashed out with the same blind recklessness. She fought with all her soul and with every trick she possessed. She had seen her fiancé Matt Rash murdered by the cattle barons. She had seen her family friend Isom Dart murdered, too. She had received threatening letters—"leave the country

Ann Bassett
Denver Public Library, Western History Collection

within 30 days or you will be killed." A full-scale range war was brewing between the small ranchers of the Hole and the larger cattle outfits. She rustled cattle from the big ranches whenever she could, especially from the Two Bar. She and her men patrolled the borders of her rangeland relentlessly. They shot any cattle that wandered onto their land or, according to Bassett legend, got them running and drove them over steep cliffs so they'd fall to their deaths.

Ann was about eleven when she saw Butch for the first time. She probably saw Elza Lay about that time, too. Over the years, each would be her beau for a time, and both Butch and Elza would remain her life-long friends. As a little girl, Ann knew that Josie had a crush on Butch, and that likely fueled her fire all the more. It was noted that while Butch helped out with the chores around the ranch, he had a shadow and her name was Ann. She followed him everywhere and made no qualms about how she felt.

When Ann was a little older, a neighbor said he saw the two girls get into a "knock-down-drag-out" fight as they argued over the outlaw's affections. As her sister's romance with Butch cooled, Ann's heated up. Rumor has it she stayed with him at his hideout to warm up the cold nights. The two sisters remained close their entire life, but they had some serious fights from time to time.

After Elza had been married and was hounded by the law, he asked Ann for a special favor because he trusted her. He gave her a map of the Powder Springs area, where he'd hidden some stolen loot. If anything happened to him, Ann was supposed to dig it up and send it to his mother. Apparently, things with his wife, Maud, were bad, and he didn't want the money going to her. Later on, when times were hard, Ann's husband, Frank Willis, was employed in oil fields that were run by Elza Lay.

Ann never lost her feistiness. In Boron, California, in the late 1930s, a circus bear turned mean and escaped into the mountains after a train derailment. At age sixty, Ann ripped down the reward poster—BEAR WANTED DEAD OR ALIVE—loaded up her Winchester, and trailed the animal for several days into the hills. She shot the animal and got her reward. In the 1950s, Ann and Frank were in Utah prospecting for uranium.

Maud Davis was Elza Lay's first wife. Elza fell head-over-heels in love with her in 1896. She lived in Vernal. Elza met her while he was working in the hay field with her brother, Albert. Albert brought the young, good-looking outlaw home, and it was love at first sight. Maud later told her daughter that she took one look at the strapping Elza and knew he was the man for her.

That fall the two were married. They lived together off and on that first year. It was an exciting adventure. Maud was whisked from place to place by bandit friends, making sure she wasn't followed by lawmen. When it was certain there was no trail, Elza would show up and take her to his hideout. It was quite an exciting ride for the young woman from Vernal. Maud must have been a rather spirited, adventuresome sort, but she would soon tire of the outlaw way.

She and Ann Bassett were close friends, according to family legend. Apparently she had known Ann before her association with the Wild Bunch. Butch and the woman he lived with at the time, either Etta Place or Ann Bassett, shared both tent and cabin with the newlyweds. There didn't seem to be any conflict among the four. Rather, they lived together happily.

Elza and Maud's grandson told Butch Cassidy biographer Pearl Baker that the four had carved their initials into the wood on the mantel at a cabin at Robber's Roost. Certainly Maud knew the truth behind the Etta/Ann mystery, but she remained tight lipped (perhaps to guard Ann's reputation). She told her children that Etta was one of the most beautiful women she'd ever seen, and she liked her quite a lot. Ann and Maud took long walks on the canyon rims together, talking and talking. They grew quite close.

Elza missed Maud while following the bandit trail. By the next year she was pregnant with their first child, and she refused to live the way she had. "It's no way to bring up a child," she said.

Both Elza and Maud were a little headstrong, and there were certainly some heated discussions about Elza changing his line of work. There were a number of close calls, too. Warrants had been issued for Elza's arrest. The law knew he was married and kept an eye on his wife and his in-laws' ranch, hoping to catch him. In the end, the pressure was too much. Maud divorced Elza.

There are unquestionably many more Wild Bunch women whose names and stories have been lost to history.

Matt Warner
The Mormon Kid

Matt Warner was born Willard Erastus Christiansen in Ephraim, Utah, in 1864, to a devoted Mormon couple. As a child, young Willard witnessed the Ephraim Indian Massacre and fled with his parents from Levan to nearby Nephi, Utah. Also as a young boy, he nearly shot a Ute brave who he thought was trying to threaten and rob his father, who ran a small store. Just before he pulled the trigger, his father told him to leave the room, that he could handle it.

The young lad wasn't much of a farmer, but he loved horses. By the time he was a teenager, he was breaking mustangs and getting paid well for it. A little later, he hired on as a cowboy with a herd being driven to Wyoming. He got as far as Roosevelt, Utah, several hundred miles away, when he realized how lovesick he was for a pretty little girl back home named Alice Sabey. He made his way back to Levan through Indian country—which in those days was still a dangerous trip.

Things were going well with the pretty Alice until a bully named Andrew Hendricksen tried to move in on Willard's true love. The fact that Andrew was a few years older than the lovesick boy didn't matter. Willard was used to making his way in the world of men, and he felt he could handle anything. One Saturday night after a church dance, the two contenders tried to walk the comely Alice to her front porch. There was a code in small Mormon towns—don't fight in front of a lady. Andrew violated the taboo. When Alice wasn't looking, he hit Willard and then reached over and tweaked his nose. When they got to Alice's gate, the poor girl, frightened of what was about to happen, ran to her door and

Matt Warner

slipped in. She favored Willard, but she wasn't sure what to do with Andrew.

As soon as the girl had shut the door, a fight erupted. The young cowboy was a quiet lad, soft-spoken mostly, and gentle, but he did have a temper when he was pushed. The fight commenced in earnest, with both boys' friends cheering them on. In anger, Willard picked up a good-sized rock and bashed the bully over the head, an act that would change the course of his life. As Andrew fell to the street, Willard tore up a bit of fence. He grabbed a post and proceeded to beat the downed lad to a pulp.

When his temper had run its course, he heard the others shouting that he had killed Andrew.

Thinking he had certainly killed the lad, he ran to his parents' house and said good-bye. He picked up his rifle and supplies, loaded up his horse, and headed north on the run. He knew if he stayed around Levan, he would be tried for murder. He was only a boy, but he was old enough to swing from hemp rope. He might even have a price on his head already. Without looking back, he headed for the cattle herd he had left.

While he was putting tracks between himself and his hometown, he ran into a freighter near Indianola and hoped to get breakfast. The man asked him what his name was. The lad had to think fast. "My name is Matt Warner," he answered. The name stuck. Years later, Willard Erastus Christiansen, when he'd paid his debt to society, gone straight, and become a lawman, decided he liked the name so much that he legally changed it.

So Matt Warner he was.

Matt Warner rode like he'd never ridden before. He made it back through Indian country, but he didn't find his herd. He found himself, at age fifteen, on Diamond Mountain outside of Vernal, Utah, on the edge of Brown's Hole. He liked the mountain plateau and took a job with a friendly rancher named Jim Warren. Jim was a good hand with stock, and he helped the young lad hone his cowboy skills. Warren also did a little rustling on the side and was good with a branding iron and a red-hot saddle ring—skills he taught his young apprentice.

The new Matt Warner had no way of knowing that the boy he'd killed wasn't really dead at all. He'd taken a horrible beating, but he recovered. The bully must have had a change of heart, since he told people that he had the beating coming for how he'd acted.

In those days, Diamond Mountain was a wild piece of real estate. Most of the folks combined ranching and rustling to make ends meet. As a cowboy, young Matt was able to hold his own with the older hands. There were a few fights, but mostly he got along. He did a man's work and got a man's pay. The other hands affectionately called him the Mormon Kid—even if he'd turned his back on many of the tenets of his childhood faith. The young Matt was good with horses and did a fair amount of breaking and training. He liked the people and the land, and with Jim Warren's help, he started a herd and built a place of his own.

Like most of the cowhands, he was continually practicing with his Colt and his Winchester in his time off—getting fast and accurate. By his own admission, he was a bit too big for his britches. Lots of drinking and gambling went on at his cabin. His carousing buddies would stop by for a party, and a lot of ranch work didn't get done.

Before he reached twenty, Matt knew too much about whiskey and games of chance—specifically poker. During this time, he got into a serious gunfight with a Mexican named Polito. Matt didn't get into trouble for this shooting, since it was considered a fair fight and no one was killed.

Matt had been lucky. In the quick-draw gun duel, Polito had been faster, but he had fired too quickly and missed. Matt was slower, but his shot was true. His bullet took the Mexican squarely in the lung. The budding young outlaw felt bad about the shooting and took the wounded man to his ranch, where he nursed him back to health.

Matt was feeling as cocky as a strutting rooster. There was a wild streak to this young man that wasn't about to be tamed. He was running with a rough crowd, and while his ranch was doing well, such a life was a little too tame for him. When his good friend and sometime-employee Elza Lay came up with a surefire way to commit the perfect crime, the aspiring desperado was an eager participant (never mind that Elza wanted a cut of the goods but didn't want to be personally involved).

As Elza explained it, an unpopular Jewish storekeeper in Wyoming had gone out of business. Before his creditors could come in and take his dry goods to auction, he'd hired a teamster to pick up the stuff in the dead of the night. He planned to take his merchandise to Vernal and sell it. Matt and his young nephew, Lew McCarty (son of the outlaw Tom McCarty), would do the robbing. It just so happened that the teamster was in on the plot, too, and played along with the holdup. Matt and his crew robbed the merchant and took his goods away on packhorses to be divided up later. The beauty of the plan was that the merchant had literally stolen the goods from his creditors, so there was no legal way he could complain without implicating himself.

This job was exciting—one more step toward the bandit trail. Like the other ranchers on Diamond Mountain and Brown's Park, Matt had done a bit of rustling and "stray gathering" to build up his herd. Now, however, his efforts got a little more organized as he drifted further and further from the straight and narrow. More and more, he left his ranch in the hands of his good friends Joe Brooks and Moroni Hendricksen, while he rode the outlaw trail. His herd of horses was doing well and growing, and he missed his ranch, but he couldn't be home for more than a week or two without becoming restless. He found himself staying away longer and longer in his outlaw adventures. He also found that his home wasn't a safe place anyway, since he was wanted by the law.

He hooked up with his brother-in-law, Tom McCarty, an old hand at the outlaw business, and another young, aspiring outlaw soon to be known as Butch Cassidy.

Matt loved horses first and foremost, so it seemed natural that he (along with his new pards) started training and racing in a five-county circuit, mostly in western Colorado. Sometimes they branched into Utah, New Mexico, and Wyoming. They had several horses that did very well—they were all excellent horsemen and good riders. By the standards of the day, they were quite successful and could have made a living from this venture, but they lived too high. They quickly drank and gambled away their race earnings. They were forced to rustle for drinking and walking-about money in the between times. They lived a fast life for cowboys. Soon they'd be called the McCarty Gang. Tom was older and more experienced, and he helped his two younger partners learn the ropes. But stealing livestock and racing just didn't bring in money fast enough.

As they sat in Tom's hideout cabin near Cortez, Colorado, passing around the Old Crow, filling their tin cups, they came up with a bold plan. They had been troublemakers, but they'd done nothing they couldn't walk away from. They wanted money and a lifestyle they couldn't seem to have as nickel-and-dime rustlers or horse-racing hustlers. They wanted the big prize.

They set their sights on the bank in Telluride, Colorado. It was a town they knew well since they'd raced their horses there. On several occasions, they'd tried their hardest to drink several of the saloons dry. They knew the setup, they knew the geography, they knew the town routines. It was a sure thing.

Dressed up like important banditos, they rode into town and robbed the bank.

There was no going back now. In spite of their efforts to keep their identities hidden, they were seen and recognized. This wasn't part of the plan. Matt and his friends were now wanted men.

Matt started watching his back trail. "While we was frying, freezing, starving, and depriving ourselves of every comfort . . . here was all that stolen money [in our money belts] . . . we couldn't go anywhere or contact anybody to spend it," Matt wrote in his 1937 autobiography, *Last of the Bandit Riders*.

Matt became acquainted with Robber's Roost and the quieter sections of Brown's Hole. Much of the romance of being a bold bandit was losing its luster. A great deal of the time was spent in the saddle, wet, cold, or hot—or scared about getting caught. A comfortable bed and a roof over your head were few and far between on the bandit trail. There were some glorious parties, where you'd buy drinks for everyone in the house, where even a large wad of money could be blown in a few days of riotous living—but there were a lot of lonely times, too, when you wondered if it was worth it. In places like Brown's Hole, it was relatively safe, and it was possible to slip back and see how your ranch was doing. But you were always a wanted man, and you could never forget it.

Later, with his friend Joe Brooks, Matt held up a store in St. Johns, Arizona. He may have held up a bank in this town, too. The pair got away with just under one thousand dollars from the store, but they picked up a serious posse that ran them all the way to the Roost.

It was a tough life, but Matt liked his fellow outlaws. He was close with Tom McCarty, Butch, and Elza Lay. He was also well liked by the folks around the Hole. Indeed, he would learn later that his friends thought enough of him to rob a bank to pay for his legal defense before he went on trial.

A man on the run doesn't like to think much about settling down—especially if it means having a good woman put her brand on him. Matt would tell his friends that a full-time woman is a liability in the bandit trade. A dance hall girl or a rented lady was as close as an outlaw should get to marriage. These were famous last words—words he'd eat when the lovebug bit him.

Enter Rose Morgan, a pretty blond with a nice personality, a curvy figure, and a lot of spunk. Sparks flew on both sides. Matt fell head-over-heels in love and took a lot of ribbing from his friends because of his past words, advice he had dished out freely to his friends on the subject of love and the outlaw way. He had egg on his face but was determined to make the relationship work. He says in his biography that Rose was eighteen, but she might have been closer to fourteen when they met. Matt was determined to settle down with this young lass and alter his life. As far as he was concerned, he was going to give up the outlaw life and go straight. Like most men, Matt was willing to lie to impress his lady love. He also conveniently forgot to tell Rose, at least in the early days, that he was an outlaw with a price on his head. Surely Rose must have figured it out before too long, but she was deeply in love and believed that he would give up his past life for a little ranch, a white picket fence, and brilliant children.

As soon as the snows melted, the lovebirds slipped over to Idaho and got married. Having to be careful, they went to Wyoming for a honeymoon. But old habits are hard to break, and there was no way to erase the price on his head or the posses that would be looking for him. Before long, Matt left his young bride and was again on the bandit trail. The two met up whenever it was safe, but the deputies weren't stupid. They knew if they kept an eye on his wife, sooner or later the husband would show up.

While Matt might have regretted the life he had chosen for himself, he always kept a good sense of humor. Perhaps the funniest joke he ever played was on Deputy Sheriff J. T. Farrer of Green River, Utah. Later on, when Matt Warner became a lawman himself, he and J. T. became close friends. Early on, though, Farrer, who was considered a hardnosed lawman, would have shot Matt on sight if he could.

There are several versions of this story. It's difficult to know where fact and legend part company. While Matt Warner's autobiography is a wonderful read, it isn't always accurate, since he sometimes plays loose with the facts. The stories and legends told about this colorful man by others "who were there" also differ. The following is a composite telling of this adventure.

One time when their supplies ran dangerously low, Butch decided to sneak down into Green River, Utah, and stock up. As much as Matt and Tom wanted to go, Green River had been their old stomping grounds, and they were afraid that they would be recognized by one of the locals. Unfortunately, Butch was spotted and quickly trailed by a posse when he left town. He did his best to trip up the lawmen, but they were good trackers. Butch picked up his partners at camp, and they hightailed it for the badlands of southern Utah.

The outlaws knew the badlands well and were able to give the posse the slip in the breaks. Matt and Butch knew where the water was, so the outlaws' canteens were full while the lawmen were not only thirsty with empty canteens but were also heading where there was no water at all. In a few hours on their present course, they would die of thirst.

Matt and Butch decided that while the posse members were out to get them, they didn't want to see them die. There was a little discussion about the wisdom of warning the lawmen, but the outlaws decided they could always shoot the deputies if they got fussy. Otherwise they'd lead them to water so they'd survive. Matt climbed up on the canyon and fired his Winchester to get the men's attention. The lawmen turned around and followed the gunshots as Matt kept out of rifle range—all the while leading the deputies to a spring by a rock slide. Matt had left a note on the trail telling the men that he was leading them to water, that the direction they had headed previously was death.

When the lawmen got to the water, they were nearly done in. They drank slowly and hydrated gradually, the way a man in that country knew was best. All along, Butch and Tom were hidden in the rocks with cocked Winchesters. Matt had his pistol drawn and was hiding behind a big rock near the men. He wanted to hear whether or not they were going to follow the bandits—even after the outlaws had saved their lives. Matt immediately recognized Sheriff Farrer and knew they might have a few troubles. He wasn't the kind to quit a trail even if the men he was trailing had rescued him from a horrid death. Apparently, the two deputies were all for turning back to town and calling it a day. The sheriff had other ideas and wouldn't hear of it. The men ate lunch after getting their fill of water. The more the sheriff talked about following the outlaws, the madder Matt got. He considered it rude to arrest a man who'd just saved him.

Without thinking, Matt jumped out from behind the rock with his Colt and told the posse to put their arms in the air. He took their guns, and when Sheriff Farrer got a little mouthy, Matt fired his pistol near his head to make the man know he meant business. The shot brought Butch and Tom out from the rocks. When the other two found out what the sheriff planned to do, they were just as angry as Matt.

With the unarmed men facing a large boulder, the three outlaws discussed what to do—a punishment must be exacted. There was serious discussion about shooting the ungrateful sheriff. Finally, Matt decided that the best thing to do would be to teach the lawmen some manners—especially that damned Sheriff Farrer.

Matt suggested sending the posse back to Green River without their pants (and guns). After a lot of protest, the lawmen were forced to loosen their britches with a few prods and threats from the outlaws. It was easy to shoot a man, but to send him back to town without his pants was a touch of class. To rub salt in the sheriff's wounds, Matt told the stubborn lawman that he was going to fly his trousers from a tree in the canyon for all to see. All the passersby would know that Matt Warner had taken Sheriff Farrer's britches.

At the last minute, the outlaws took the sheriff's saddle, too, but let his two subordinates keep theirs. Legend has it that the sheriff had some pretty baggy drawers, and the trapdoor didn't have a button. Before long he also had a sore backside from riding bareback. In fact, his bottom was so sore that he had to walk his mount a good part of the way. When the good sheriff finally stumbled back into Green River, he was, well, the butt of a lot of jokes. The sheriff had refused to ride in one of his men's saddles. Before he got to town, he is reputed to have said, "It won't hurt the people around here to see a man without his pants." Sheriff Farrer

Matt Warner (back right) poses with gunfighters Jack Egan (standing left),
Mid Nichols (seated left), and attorney Mark Braffett

wanted to nail Butch and Matt to the wall, but he took the ignominy with dignity and humor.

For a time Matt took his robbery act north. He robbed the bank at Roslyn, Washington, a few days before his child was born. He could have gotten away with nearly twenty thousand dollars. But Rose's sister was a feisty woman. She'd had enough of Rose being married to a bandit. She tipped off the law, and Matt was finally caught. With a lot of legal trickery and a lot of money placed in the right hands, he managed to walk away from the charges. But he was having second thoughts about the outlaw life.

After a few more scrapes, his luck ran out. On May 5, 1896, he was arrested and jailed for a shooting, which he claims was self-defense (and it probably was). Things went from bad to worse. In June Rose gave birth to a boy named Rex LeRoy Christiansen (named after Butch Cassidy). In September Matt and William Wall were convicted of manslaughter, and he was looking at hard jail time. He was sentenced to the Utah State Prison. A few days later Rose died of bone cancer.

In January 1900 Matt Warner and Wall were released from prison and pardoned. Shortly after they were released, they were arrested in Vernal. The charges were dropped. In 1902 Matt married a girl named Elma Zufelt from Green River. It was a good match. Settling down in Price, Utah, Matt became a lawman and later a justice of the peace.

The following is written on Matt Warner's memorial plaque at the Carbon County Courthouse in Price, Utah.

MATT WARNER
APRIL 12, 1864–DECEMBER 21, 1935

THE BANDIT WHO BECAME JUDGE
Matt Warner was born Willard E. Christiansen
In Ephraim, Utah. He left home at the age

Of 14 after a fight in which he thought he
Killed the town bully. He took the name Matt
Warner, became a cattle rustler, bank robber,
And rode with Butch Cassidy until going to
Prison on trumped up charges in 1897. He was
Released in 1900, with a full pardon from
Governor Well. In the following years, he
Became one of the best deputy sheriffs, city
Police officers, and justices of the peace
Carbon County has ever known. As a man of
The law, Warner won the love of all Carbon
County, except the lawyers, and stuffed shirts.
He was strictly a man of the people.

──Gunplay Maxwell──
The Wannabe Gunman

Gunplay Maxwell wasn't getting the respect he deserved. He'd offered his services to several outlaw gangs, but they'd turned him down cold. No one was taking him seriously. The problem was respect—or rather a lack of respect for his abilities as an outlaw. It was also showing up among the residents in the local towns. He couldn't have folks thinking he wasn't good enough. Even the Wild Bunch had rejected him.

Not far from the sleepy town of Green River, Utah, Gunplay rode up a small hill. He was fuming mad. Near the summit, he came upon a wagon driven by a couple of sodbusters who were taking a load of fresh-cut prairie hay to town. Gunplay decided these bumpkins would be the perfect candidates for some, well, gunplay. He'd teach these farm boys a thing or two. It might help reestablish his waning reputation. As was customary in that day, a few pleasantries were exchanged as the horseman and the wagon met. Then Gunplay's expression changed as he loosened his pistol and told the two they were going to learn how to dance to the sound of Samuel Colt.

At the brandishing of the .45, the sodbusters reluctantly got down from the wagon. Maxwell explained the game and began shooting near their feet. The farmers started doing the Gunplay two-step as the heavy lead bullets tore into the hard ground too close for comfort. This would teach folks in these parts to tread on his reputation. Gunplay was amused as the two farmers did the jig. The dancing men were no doubt hoping this madman was a good shot—those slugs were coming mighty close.

Gunplay hadn't noticed that another farmer had been sleeping in the back of the wagon. All the shooting had spoiled his nap. This fellow, no doubt cranky and irritable at being disturbed, snuck out of the wagon and grabbed the weapon from the "bad man" when he wasn't looking. Then, in anger, the cranky farmer pulled Gunplay off his horse and slammed him headfirst into the hard, red dirt. Gunplay no longer held the aces. He wasn't much of a hand-to-hand man. Fistfighting, after all, was beneath him—he was trying to be a famous gunman, not a common country brawler.

Three very angry Green River sodbusters faced the unarmed gunman with the intent of doing some busting of their own. The dancing had warmed them up. They took turns beating the sorry gunfighter looking for a reputation. They punched him several dozen times to get his attention, then they pistol-whipped him with his own Colt to make sure he really understood. To drive the lesson home, they beat him some more. Then they pistol-whipped him again—thinking poor Gunplay was getting what he so richly deserved. He was pounded nearly to death for his bad manners—and it wouldn't be the last time.

The gunman couldn't be revived for another thumping, so the farmers slumped his punched, kicked, and pistol-whipped body over his horse and sent him down the road feeling he'd gotten off lucky. The beating surely didn't do his reputation any good.

Gunplay wanted to be respected for his criminal prowess—respected like Butch Cassidy, Matt Warner, or Elza Lay. He wanted to be known as a lightning-quick gunman like Billy the Kid, Kid Curry, John Hardin, or the Sundance Kid. He'd coined the catchy handle "Gunplay" so folks would know he meant business. He wanted to be an outlaw, but most of all he wanted to be known as a deadly gunfighter.

No doubt, most intelligent outlaws quickly saw that he'd never be more than a mean-spirited, petty man. They realized that his lack of judgment and his thirst for a reputation were the sort of things that could get a man killed on a job. An outlaw wanting to stay in business was concerned with pulling the job and getting away with his skin intact. Gangs weren't looking for a wannabe member to provide comic relief.

Near Nine Mile Canyon, Gunplay ran a penny-ante rustling operation—stealing a few cows from some of the bigger ranches. It was quite small compared to some of the larger rustling operations in the area. His brother, who changed his name to avoid suspicion, had opened up a butcher shop in Price. Gunplay supplied him with all the beef he could cut. This trade paid enough to keep the aspiring gunman in whiskey, but it wasn't the romantic life he'd pictured for himself as a bad man. A fellow establishing a bloody reputation didn't steal beef for a butcher shop.

Being a petty thief was wearing on Gunplay. If he couldn't pull off a big job, at least he could bully someone or pick a gunfight with a family man—this at least made him feel better. He hoped it would also make others think he was a real tough guy. In an angry mood, he rode near the Green River after a botched rustling episode. He smelled fire and coffee. As was the custom, he greeted the camp. In those days, even aspiring gunmen didn't walk up to a campfire unannounced. It was a good way to catch some unwanted lead.

The friendly folks at the camp naturally invited him in. They were a bunch of good-natured miners prospecting for gold in the rugged canyons. After downing a heaping plateful of beef and beans and several cups of steaming coffee, Gunplay got to bragging about what a pistol fighter he was. Worse, he started picking on one of the miners—a small, quiet man.

This was a serious breach of western etiquette. When you were invited to a fire and fed, you owed your host some courtesy. You didn't go on the prod for a fight. That was the height of bad manners.

All the miners had rifles, but none were packing six-guns. Apparently, the rifles weren't quite handy. After a fair amount of abuse, the miners invited Gunplay to take off his Colts. One of them would fight him bare knuckle. Of course, he said no. He was a gunman not a lowly fistfighter. He continued pushing the small miner, who refused a gunfight—the miner knew nothing about handguns and the fast draw. Many of the group thought that Gunplay was going to shoot the poor unarmed man to make his point. Finally, one of the miners saw his chance and grabbed the gunman's arms. Gunplay was quickly stripped of his weapon.

The small miner now took his turn. Without ceremony, the little fellow beat the stuffing out of Gunplay Maxwell. The miner might have been small, but he was strong and quick—and he was also mad. Legend has it that Gunplay never connected with a single hit of his own. The miner punched the gunman's face until it was a bloody pulp. Then he punched it again. Before it was over, Maxwell's nose was a little out of place, and he was bleeding heavily. After that, the miner started working on Gunplay's stomach and back. Gunplay was beaten nearly to death. The miners slumped Gunplay Maxwell's badly pummeled body on his horse and sent him on his way half-dead. They told him to come back if he wanted more.

Gunplay had a habit of pushing too far and forgetting the last beating he'd earned. He couldn't keep his big mouth shut. Gunplay was in the Vernal area when he almost got fitted for a new set of wings (or maybe horns)—this time by none other than the good-natured Butch Cassidy. This was one of the rare times Gunplay picked a fight with someone who could fight back. Gunplay was liquored up in a mining camp on the outside of town. He was winning a few hands of poker, which was unusual, and feeling extra aggressive. Bragging to the miners, he said the Maxwell Gang was getting powerful and would soon replace the Wild Bunch (he was still bitter over being blackballed by the outfit he wanted to join the most). After a few more drinks, he said Vernal and Brown's Hole weren't big enough for the two of them.

He further boasted that Butch Cassidy had one day to get out of town or he was going to gun for him.

He probably wasn't aware that Butch was also in town that day. Maybe Gunplay was too drunk to care. It didn't take long for this talk to get back to Butch. Butch didn't take to this sort of bragging and knew it had to be stopped here and now. He called Gunplay Maxwell out. Butch must have been very angry, since he prided himself on never killing a man. Apparently he'd make an exception with this braggart—or he knew how much backbone the man really had. There are several stories about what actually happened.

One is that the two men rode toward each other with their Colt pistols drawn. Another is that they rode toward one another with their pistols holstered, planning to draw when the time came. The last version says they walked toward each other until they could nearly touch.

Whatever happened, they ended up quite close to each other—close enough to hear a whisper. All the stories say that Butch leaned over and said something near Gunplay's ear. Butch meant to shoot and Gunplay knew it. He also knew that he'd have no chance against Butch, who was very fast and a crack shot. Butch never killed anyone, but Gunplay knew he could if he wanted to. The aspiring bad guy must have known that he was outgunned. With his tail between his legs, Gunplay rode out of town disgraced, but alive. Legend has it that Butch said something about a funeral about to take place in Vernal and that it would be Gunplay's if he didn't walk (or ride) straight out of town immediately. Butch supposedly said, "This town isn't big enough for the two of us."

Gunplay decided to start up an actual Maxwell Gang and go into the bank robbery business. The Wild Bunch had since left the country, and the playing field was wide open. The gang headed for Provo to make their names in the big-league world of high-stakes crime. However, someone in the gang (likely Gunplay himself) had drunk too much whiskey. Reed Smoot, the owner of the Provo Bank, was tipped off. He doubled the guard and moved the cash just to be on the safe side.

Disappointed, but not completely out of the game, the Maxwell Gang decided on a whim to hit the bank in Springville. With little more than a cursory plan, the gang traveled a few miles south to make their mark. The gang was overly confident and did a poor job of casing the joint.

For some unexplained reason, two of the gang rented a buggy for a getaway vehicle. Outside of town, near Hobble Creek Canyon, these two Maxwell Gang members were also supposed to have several horses waiting. Perhaps the robbers thought the buggy looked less obtrusive in a quiet town. Had the gang had horses instead of the buggy, their plan might have worked.

Gunplay chose a man named Porter to go into the bank with him. Porter didn't have much between his ears, but Gunplay was very anxious to get on with the robbery. On a Saturday morning, he walked into the bank. It was a pleasant May day on the Wasatch Front. Proud of his new job status as bank robber and the head of his own gang, Gunplay stuck a Colt revolver in the cashier's face. While Porter covered the man, Gunplay went into the cage and started collecting the loot. In his eagerness, he was clumsy. Several times he dropped stacks of twenties on the ground—then bent down to pick them up. He was one excited bad boy. Porter was smiling, too. They were going to be filthy rich. Porter took his eyes off the cashier when Gunplay dropped another stack of bills. He loved looking at the money. The cashier managed to slip his hand under the counter and press an alarm button that sounded in Reynolds Hardware across the street.

When the alarm went off in the hardware store, Reynolds figured it was a false alarm. They'd happened before. Still, he decided he'd better check. Reynolds picked up his phone and called the bank to be sure. It seemed strange that no one answered, and that worried him. At the bank, the ringing phone rattled Gunplay, and he lost his nerve. He took the money, and he and Porter made a run for the buggy.

Reynolds, who was watching out the window, saw this happen and reached for a handy Winchester. He fired a shot or two while the cashier ran out the front door of the bank yelling that there'd been a robbery. Being a good citizen, Reynolds jumped in his cumbersome old lumber wagon and took off after the robbers in the racing buggy.

Gunplay realized, too late, that the buggy was a mistake. On the edge of town, he and Porter ran into a man named Snelson riding a powerful bay horse. Gunplay offered to buy the animal on the spot. Snelson refused to sell. Gunplay and Porter stuck six-guns in his face and pulled him off the bay. Gunplay threw forty-six dollars at the man for the mount. In the meantime, the heavy lumber wagon had about caught up with the stumbling outlaws. Reynolds climbed down and fired a few more rounds in their direction.

In some accounts, Gunplay mounted the horse, leaving Porter to drive the buggy. In other accounts, both men tried to mount the horse together.

Trying to buy the horse had taken more time than the desperados had. Springville might have been a sleepy Utah town, but the citizens could rally well in an emergency, and they came well armed. A posse of mounted men (some accounts say firing weapons as they rode) passed the lumber wagon at a dead gallop. Some men dismounted and joined Reynolds, firing. The oak and buck brush was thick by the side of the road. The outlaws left the horse and buggy, grabbed the money, and dove into the thick cover. They would have been easy targets on the road. Running for a short distance, the two split up and found places to hide.

The posse, on hands and knees in some sections, made a skirmish line and pushed through the heavy brush. Gunplay didn't do a good job of hiding. Before long he was looking into the barrels of Mormon Winchester rifles and scatterguns. He gave up without incident. He had $3,085.50 on his person. (Nearly six hundred dollars from the robbery was never found.)

Porter wasn't so lucky. He pushed farther into the thick brush, vowing that he wasn't going down easy. He started shooting at the posse closing in on him. He hit J. W. Allen just above the knee with a lucky shot. Allen fell. From the ground, he got a good look at Porter in his hiding place. Steadying his rifle on his elbow, Allen took aim. He put a bullet through the outlaw's head. Porter died instantly. Allen's leg ailed for the rest of his life.

Gunplay Maxwell was sent to prison for his crimes. He served only two years, one of the luckiest breaks of his life.

Around 1910, he was still up to his usual tricks in eastern Utah. There are two eyewitness accounts of how Gunplay Maxwell met his end.

The first, and most interesting, says Gunplay met a man called Shoot 'Em Up Bill in a Price bar. They were both whiskey drinkers, braggarts looking to make a name. Each pushed a little too far. After a bit of drinking and bragging, a deadly challenge was issued. They met on Main Street for an old-fashioned shootout at high noon. Both men went for their guns. Shoot 'Em Up Bill was a lot faster. He fired two shots. Gunplay is reported to have stood there, not sure what to do. Apparently he had cleared leather but never got off a round. Finally, Gunplay dropped to the dirt, two rounds through his chest.

The other story is less romantic. Maxwell and Shoot 'Em Up Bill probably would have shot it out sooner or later. They hated each other and had exchanged threats. Before the two could shoot it out, though, someone else beat Bill to it. Gunplay was drinking too much in Price and didn't have his wits about him while he was talking. There was a fight of some sort. He was killed by a guard from the Castle Gate Mine (the same mine Butch and Elza had robbed a little more than a decade before).

He was probably shot—although he could have been stabbed or beaten. Either way, Gunplay Maxwell met his end. He'd be pleased to know that his reputation has lived into the next century.

Joe Walker
The Old Guy Outlaw

Being a bad guy had short-term rewards: wine, women, and song. And there was adventure. But the retirement compensations weren't so promising.

Being an outlaw was mostly a young man's trade. A outlaw usually died hard and broke—never getting near retirement age. Joe Walker was an old man by outlaw standards. He was in his forties when he took up with the Wild Bunch, a fair-looking man, dark and a bit sultry. Today Joe Walker might be called a silent gent, maybe a bit sullen, one who minded his own business.

He did what was expected of him and considered Butch Cassidy a capable leader. Joe was the third man on the famous Castle Gate payroll robbery. He cut the wires out of the canyon leading to Price, and he was the man Butch trusted with the money. The posses thought only two men had been involved in the robbery (Butch Cassidy and Elza Lay)—they weren't looking for a third man. Near Desert Lake, Joe took the seven thousand dollars in gold and hightailed it back to the hideout, while the other two led the posses on a merry chase across some of the more desolate parts of Utah. When Butch and Elza got back to Robber's Roost, Joe was there with the gold.

Joe Walker wasn't a bad man. He mostly turned outlaw by circumstance. He felt cheated out of his family inheritance, and that made him bitter. So he did something about it—even if it wasn't legal.

The respectable Whitmore family from Carbon County were important folks, with extensive banking and ranching interests in the area.

Joe's uncle was the Whitmore family patriarch. When Joe's father died, this uncle managed the family cattle—half of which belonged to Joe's immediate family. It was understood that a share would go to the dead brother's children when they came of age.

When Joe's uncle was killed in Arizona a few years later during an Indian raid, the rest of the family moved the herd north and started a new life in Utah. When Joe came of age, he rode north to claim some of the herd, or at least an interest in the operation he felt was partly his. He wanted to start his own ranch. He didn't expect a lot. The Whitmores had turned the herd into a small fortune. Joe felt he was owed something since his father's cattle had been the basis of the initial operation.

His Whitmore cousins, told him he didn't have a valid claim and needed to leave. In retrospect, it probably would have been cheaper for his cousins to have given him some cattle or money. Perhaps if his uncle had been alive, things would have been different. Instead, they treated their cousin rudely and all but threw him out as an interloper and a freeloader.

Joe Walker was bitter, but he tried again. The results were the same.

He was determined to get even and made rustling Whitmore cattle and horses his life's business. Joe led numerous raids on their assets, costing them thousands of dollars in livestock losses and wasted man-hours. Some legends say he even married one of the Whitmore daughters to get back at his cousins, but this doesn't seem likely.

The Whitmore family had a lot of clout. They wrote to the governor and other officials about placing a higher price on Cousin Joe's head. They also helped put up some of the reward money for his capture—dead or alive—and underwrote the cost of several posses. Due to their influence, at one time Joe was listed as one of the twelve most undesirable men in the Roost.

Joe Walker had a streak of mean when crossed. His family had crossed him, and they would pay dearly. Besides cattle, the Whitmore folks prided themselves on their premium horseflesh. Joe appreciated stock, and what was theirs became his. On one occasion, he took three very valuable horses and used them to pay a debt to one of the Whitmores' friends. This didn't set well with either party.

Joe was a good shot with a rifle or pistol. He was also a fine cowboy and a good hand. Sometimes whiskey drinking, though, got the best of him. In 1895, after a few too many drinks over the line, Joe decided the best thing to do was shoot up the town of Price. After nearly killing some prominent citizens and destroying property, he left in a hurry. Not long after that, under the influence of rotgut at his favorite watering hole, Joe tried to shoot a fellow named Milburn who tried to push him around.

Joe got wind that he was about to be arrested for attempted murder, so he left as fast as he could cinch the saddle down on his horse. He headed for a cabin on the Colorado River, where he could lie low while things in Price cooled down. After that, he headed to Robber's Roost, a place he knew well.

Joe Walker never had anything good to say about Gunplay Maxwell. Joe would not ride with Gunplay and no doubt was part of the Wild Bunch's blackballing of the aspiring outlaw who desperately wanted a reputation. Perhaps as revenge, Gunplay joined up with a posse to lead Sheriff Tuttle into the Roost to find Joe. He took the lawmen to one of Joe's favorite camps, a small canyon called Mexican Bend. Personal differences aside, this was a violation of bad-guy ethics. Joe's only thought was to shoot the traitor—he could deal with the posses afterward.

Joe was a good shot, but he waited until Gunplay was 50 yards away. When he had him dead in his sights, Joe took up the slack in his trigger, took a breath, and squeezed. However, it was a lucky day for Gunplay. The bullet hit the barrel on his Winchester—ruining the rifle but saving his life. Gunplay dove for the rocks, shaken but alive. It wasn't a good day for Sheriff Tuttle, however, who caught a round near the hip, a very painful injury.

Joe fired some shots to keep the men pinned down. Tuttle was in bad shape, but the cowardly Gunplay and the other like-minded posse members snuck off in the dark, leaving the suffering sheriff to fend for himself during the night. The next morning they returned, surprised to find Tuttle alive. The sheriff was finally given medical help, but he nearly died from his wounds. Gunplay had slipped away.

Joe felt bad about shooting the sheriff. He liked the man. He blamed Gunplay for the incident.

If Joe had not been shot, he likely would have called out Gunplay Maxwell. However, Joe had pushed his luck too far and had too many enemies. Even Governor Wells of Utah had offered a five-hundred-dollar reward for him. He was wanted dead or alive.

In April 1898, a group of sheriffs and marshals were hot on Joe's trail. In the posse was Jack Watson, a famous tracker from Colorado; Sheriff Allred from Price, who had signed warrants; Joe Bush, a famous U.S. deputy marshal; other ranchers, including Joe's cousins, the Whitmores; and other lawmen—thirteen in all.

Jim McPherson, a local rancher, was drafted as a guide. He was a friend of the Wild Bunch and didn't want to make the trip—but he agreed to come when a Colt was pointed at him. As the posse would discover, he made the difference, since he knew how the outlaws thought and where they laid over.

All things considered, it was an impressive group.

In the past, posses had been thrown off by local sympathizers who weren't eager to see the law succeed. Loyalties rested with the Wild Bunch. Besides, the posse usually didn't know the country the way an outlaw did. Joe Walker's trail led into the rugged Book Cliff Mountains, a distance south of Brown's Hole. The posse was nearly out of food, and worse, coffee, when the trail got hot. They pushed on ahead with half rations and were very close to capturing Joe Walker and his cohorts. They could have stopped and hunted up a deer or an antelope, but Joe Bush could taste success in his mouth and kept pushing his men.

Near Florence Creek, some time after midnight, scouts came upon

Joe Walker's camp. The posse made a cold camp about a mile from the outlaws. About an hour before dawn, the lawmen crept close to the sleeping outlaw camp. There are several firsthand versions of what happened on this cool spring morning in the Book Cliffs. One account has four men rolled up in their blankets. Apparently, the bandits thought they had eluded the posse. Their fire was still glowing since someone had stoked it in the middle of the night. A rock face reflected the fire. The horses were tied up about 40 yards away on a picket line. Off to one side there was a deep gully.

After the lawmen were in place, Joe Bush identified himself and his posse and told the sleeping outlaws to surrender or be killed. He called for them to put down their guns or they'd go in over their saddles. Joe Bush was known for being a no-nonsense lawman. He gave a fellow just one chance to go in breathing. If that someone turned down the offer, Joe didn't think twice about putting a bullet in him. He meant business.

Two outlaws gave up and reached high.

Another man grabbed his gun and fired as he tried to make it to the gully. With thirteen Winchesters on him, he was shot dead before he could get more than a foot or two from his bedroll. Joe Walker wasn't about to give up without a fight. He fired his six-gun at the lawmen, who in turn opened fire on him. In the resulting volley of fire, Joe Walker was shot a number of times, but a bullet in his heart killed him the fastest. The lawmen figured they fired over fifty bullets in less than a minute.

Joe Walker was brought out of the Book Cliff Mountains wrapped in his blanket, tied to his saddle.

Another account is a little different. It suggests that the Joe Bush posse actually wasn't after Joe Walker at this time at all. Rather, the lawmen thought they were hot on the trail of Butch Cassidy or the Sundance Kid. Since the two more famous outlaws were known for shooting their way out of tight corners (which isn't necessarily true), the lawmen crept in on the sleeping men and decided it might be better to shoot first and talk later. Since they thought they had these two wanted men in a compromising situation, they weren't going to let them get away. In this account, there were only two men (not four). Without a customary warning or an identification, the lawmen shot into the sleeping men's bedrolls without mercy. Surprise: There was no Butch and Sundance, but a dead Joe Walker. In the lawmen's opinion, he wasn't a bad second best.

Either way, the outlaw Joe Walker would never steal Whitmore cattle again.

Further Reading

Armstrong, Erma. "Aunt Ada and the Outlaws: The Story of C. L. Maxwell." *Outlaw Trail Journal*, Winter 1997.

Baker, Pearl. *The Wild Bunch at Robbers Roost*. New York: Abelard-Schuman, 1971. Reprint, Lincoln: University of Nebraska Press, 1989.

————. *Robber's Roost Recollections*. Logan: Utah State University Press, 1976.

Betenson, Bill. "Lula Parker Betenson." *Outlaw Trail Journal*, Winter 1995.

Betenson, Lula, and Dora Flack. *Butch Cassidy, My Brother*. Provo, Utah: Brigham Young University Press, 1975.

Briehan, Carl W. *Wild Women of the West*. New York: New American Library, 1982.

Brown, Dee. *The American West*. New York: Charles Scribner's Sons, 1994.

Buck, Daniel, and Anne Meadows. *Digging Up Butch and Sundance*. Rev. ed. Lincoln, Neb.: Bison Books, 1996.

————. "Etta Place: A Most Wanted Woman." *Western Outlaw-Lawman History Association Journal*, Spring-Summer 1993.

————. "Etta Place: Wild Bunch Mystery Lady." *The English Westerners' Society Tally Sheet*, Spring 1993.

————. "Showdown at San Vincente." *True West*, February 1993.

————. "Where Lies Butch Cassidy?" *Old West*, Fall 1991.

Burroughs, John Rolfe. *Where the Old West Stayed Young*. New York: William Morrow and Company, 1962.

Burton, Doris Karren. "Charley Crouse's Robbers' Roost." *Outlaw Trail Journal*, Winter 1993.

Carlson, Chip. *Tom Horn: Blood on the Moon*. Glendo, Wyo.: High Plains Press, 2001.

————. "The Tipton Train Robbery," *Western Outlaw-Lawman History Association Journal*, Summer 1995.

Churchill, Richard. *The McCarty's*. Leadville, Co.: Timberline Books, 1972.

DeJournette, Dick, and Jan DeJournette. *One Hundred Years of Brown's Park and Diamond Mountain*. Vernal, Utah: Mansfield Printing, Inc.,1996.

Drago, Gail. *Etta Place: Her Life and Times with Butch Cassidy and the Sundance Kid*. Plano, Tex.: Republic of Texas Press, 1996.

Dullenty, Jim. *The Butch Cassidy Collection*. Hamilton, Mont.: Rocky Mountain House Press, 1986.

————. "The Farm Boy Who Became a Member of Butch Cassidy's Wild Bunch." *Quarterly of the National Association and Center for Outlaw and Lawmen History*, Winter 1986.

Ernst, Donna B. "Black Gold and the Wild Bunch." *Quarterly of the National Association and Center for Outlaw and Lawmen History*, March 1994.

————. "Friends of the Pinkertons." *Quarterly of the National Association and Center for Outlaw and Lawmen History*, June 1995.

————. *From Cowboy to Outlaw: The True Story of Will Carver*. Sonora, Tex.: Sutton County Historical Society, 1995.

————. "The Sundance Kid: Wyoming Cowboy. *Western Outlaw-Lawman History Association Journal*, Spring 1992.

Hampton, Wade. "Brigandage on Our Railroads." *North American Review*, December 1893.

Hayden, Willard C. "Butch Cassidy and the Great Montpelier Bank Robbery." *Idaho Yesterdays*, Spring 1971.

Horan, James. *The Wild Bunch*. New York: Signet Books, 1958.

Kelsey, Michael R. *Hiking and Exploring Utah's Henry Mountains and Robbers Roost*, Provo Utah: Kelsey Publishing, 1990.

Kildare, Maurice. "Bear River Loot." *Real West*, September 1968.

Kouris, Diana. *Romantic and Notorious History of Brown's Park*. Basin, Wyo.: Wolverine Gallery, 1988.

————. "The Lynching Calamity in Brown's Park." *True West*, September 1995.

Larson, T. A. *History of Wyoming*. Lincoln: University of Nebraska Press, 1965.

Lavender, David. *The Telluride Story*. Ridgeway, Colo.: Wayfinder Press, 1987.

McCarty, Tom. *Tom McCarty's Own Story*. Hamilton, Mont.: Rocky Mountain House Press, 1986.

McClure, Grace. *The Bassett Women*. Athens, Ohio: Swallow Press/Ohio University Press, 1985.

Meadows, Anne. *Digging Up Butch and Sundance*. New York: St. Martin's Press, 1994.

Morn, Frank. *The Eye That Never Sleeps: A History of the Pinkertons National Detective Agency*. Bloomington: Indiana University Press, 1982.

Patterson, Richard. *Butch Cassidy: A Biography*. Lincoln: University of Nebraska Press, 1998.

———. "Did the Sundance Kid Take Part in the Telluride Robbery?" *Western Outlaw-Lawman History Association Journal*, Summer 1994.

———. *Historical Atlas of the Outlaw West*. Boulder: Johnson Books, 1985.

———. *The Train Robbery Era: An Encyclopedic History*. Boulder: Pruett Publishing, 1991.

Pointer, Larry. *In Search of Butch Cassidy*. Norman: University of Oklahoma Press, 1977.

Redford, Robert. *The Outlaw Trail, A Journey Through Time*. New York: Grosset & Dunlap, 1976.

Selcer, Richard F. *Hell's Half Acre: The Life and Legend of a Red-Light District*. Fort Worth: Texas Christian University Press, 1991.

Slatta, Richard W. "The Legendary Butch and Sundance." *The Mythical West: An Encyclopedia of Legend, Lore, and Popular Culture*. Santa Barbara, Calif.: ABC-CLIO, 2001.

Stegner, Wallace. *Mormon Country*. New York: Hawthorne Books, 1942.

Walker, Herb. *Butch Cassidy*. Amarillo: Baxter Lane Company, 1975.

Warner, Matt (as told to Murray E. King). *The Last of the Bandit Riders*. New York: Bonanza Books, 1938. Reprint 1950.

Index